Oasis

Conversion Stories
of Hollywood Legends

MARY CLAIRE KENDALL

*Wishing you
an oasis of
faith & healing.*
Mary Claire Kendall
6/21/15

Franciscan
MEDIA
Cincinnati, Ohio

Cover and book design by Mark Sullivan

Cover images: © Veer | Adamson; Veer | CarolPhoto; iStock | Gemenacom

LIBRARY OF CONGRESS CATALOGING-IN-PUBLICATION DATA
Kendall, Mary Claire, 1959-
Oasis : conversion stories of Hollywood legends / Mary Claire Kendall ; foreword by Dolores Hart.
pages cm
Includes bibliographical references.
ISBN 978-1-61636-861-6 (paperback)
1. Catholic converts—United States—Biography. 2. Entertainers—United States—Religious life. I. Title.
BX4668.A1K46 2015
248.2'420922—dc23
[B]
2015003935

ISBN 978-1-61636-861-6

Published by Franciscan Media
28 W. Liberty St.
Cincinnati, OH 45202
www.FranciscanMedia.org

Printed in the United States of America.
Printed on acid-free paper.
15 16 17 18 19 5 4 3 2 1

Contents

DEDICATION | v

FOREWORD | vii

PREFACE | ix

ACKNOWLEDGMENTS | xiii

INTRODUCTION | xv

CHAPTER ONE | 1
 All Too Human: The Need for Healing and Recovery

CHAPTER TWO | 15
 Alfred Hitchcock Comes Full Circle (1899–1980)

CHAPTER THREE | 23
 Gary Cooper's Quiet Journey of Faith (1901–1961)

CHAPTER FOUR | 37
 Bob Hope and His Ladies of Hope (1903–2003)

CHAPTER FIVE | 51
 Mary Astor: Becoming a Star...and a Saint (1906–1987)

CHAPTER SIX | 75
 John Wayne's Longest Journey (1907–1979)

CHAPTER SEVEN | 89
 Ann Sothern: Surviving with Optimism and Faith (1909–2001)

CHAPTER EIGHT | 97
 How Jane Wyman Dealt with Tragedy (1917–2007)

CHAPTER NINE | 107
Susan Hayward: From Brooklyn to Bountiful (1917–1975)

CHAPTER TEN | 123
Lana Turner: Finding God and Security—Within (1921–1995)

CHAPTER ELEVEN | 139
Betty Hutton's Miraculous Recovery (1921–2007)

CHAPTER TWELVE | 157
Ann Miller's Quest for Spiritual Gold (1923–2004)

CHAPTER THIRTEEN | 169
Patricia Neal's Dramatic Journey of Faith, Healing, and Forgiveness (1926–2010)

CONCLUSION | 185

BIBLIOGRAPHY | 187

NOTES | 192

Dedication

This book is dedicated to my great-grandmother Lillian Webster Keane (1878–1965), who converted to Catholicism as a little girl.

Lillian wrote in her diary that the faith "lightened the burdens of life."[1]

When I told my mother on Holy Saturday 2014, my decision regarding the book's dedication, she was delighted.

Lillian raised her granddaughter, and my mother, after her daughter Helena died at age thirty-three, while cradling her six-month-old baby, Claire, in her arms.

Tragically, and coincidentally, my mother died some three months later on Tuesday, July 15, 2014, the forty-ninth anniversary of her grandmother's death.

And so, I dedicate this book to my mother, Claire Yvonne Biberstein Kendall (1932–2014), as well—with love and gratitude.

Foreword

My entire life as a child growing up in a movie-star-conscious family was focused on one thing: How can I participate in this world? By the age of seven, I had decided God must help me to become a movie star. My teenage parents had been summoned to Hollywood by a talent scout and their journey ended up bringing Daddy's sister and her new husband, Johnny, to Hollywood, too. Johnny had the voice everyone bragged about, and, as with so many of the stars Mary Claire writes of, Hollywood changed his name to craft just the right image. He would be called "Mario Lanza."

Along my own journey to Hollywood, I went to every movie I could possibly see with my grandfather, who was a projectionist in a Chicago theater, with whom I stayed, along with grandmother, until I was old enough to join my Hollywood family. I watched every great actor and actress in the forties and fifties. So reading Mary Claire's book was like "old home week" to me—so many years later. But part of the reason I love her work is that I finally did get my wish to become an actress. That's for another book, which Mary Claire promises to write. And I'll hold her to it.

The twelve stars she has chosen for this book resonate with me because somehow or another I worked with or met or became friends with the folks she writes about. Maria Cooper Janis, the daughter of Gary, became my closest friend. Mr. Hitchcock gave me my first TV acting job. I got strangled in the first act but I would do it again for Hitchcock—in a heartbeat. Patricia Neal was sent to our Abbey after her husband Roald Dahl kicked her out of their marriage. By this time I was in the Abbey of Regina Laudis and received this other great lady as a friend for life, even burying her after her death in our own cemetery.

In short, I can not only encourage you to read Mary Claire's book, I can recommend it from the heart as a beautiful journal of people I have loved and respected. Mary Claire also loves and respects the people she has brought back to us in her book. This is clear. She inhabits their lives, their journeys of film and faith as she vividly brings them to life.

Anyone who has grown up in those golden years of movie-making will find their own reason to cheer and weep and celebrate the stars who no longer shine in a new age of filmmaking. Take her book home with you as a precious book of historical views, of memories and of your own journal of the Hollywood that began Hollywood. With gratitude to Mary Claire Kendall.

Mother Dolores Hart, Prioress
Abbey of Regina Laudis
Bethlehem, Connecticut

Preface

One night, I stumbled upon the amazing Betty Hutton.

It was October 17, 2006. Turner Classic Movies was rebroadcasting her 2000 interview with Robert Osbourne. It was also the third anniversary of the death of a good friend, who had died of Lou Gehrig's. A good omen, I thought. In February 2007, I wrote to Betty, requesting an interview. But she was not long for this world, dying on March 11, 2007. So I wrote her story for *Our Sunday Visitor*. Soon, *Newport Life Magazine* green-lighted her story, as well, and before long I was interviewing A.C. Lyles, longtime Paramount producer, about Betty. He had started out as Adolph Zukor's "office boy" in 1936, soon rising to Director of Publicity, then producer—as well as Ronald Reagan's best friend. He was also great friends of Betty—Paramount's biggest star in the forties—and had given her eulogy. When I called, to my surprise, A.C. called back within hours, graciously offering me an interview the very next day, Friday, June 15. Coincidentally, that was the day that Spencer Tracy's son John would die.

On July 6, when I called A.C. for a follow-up interview, he had just delivered John Tracy's eulogy and suggested I make him my next story.

That September, Fr. C. John McCloskey emailed me with news of Jane Wyman's death, writing, "Another conversion story for you." I dug right in, and *Our Sunday Visitor* immediately ran my piece.

By January 2008, my mother began suggesting I write a book profiling these celebrity faith journeys.

Next, A.C. introduced me to Maria Cooper Janis, the daughter of Gary Cooper, after I spoke with him on February 6, 2008—Reagan's birthday, no less—when he vividly recounted Coop's breakout role in *Wings* (1928), the first Oscar-winning picture.

That April, I interviewed Maria at her Park Avenue apartment and finished "Gary Cooper's Quiet Journey of Faith" by July 4. Then Maria suggested I consider writing about her friend Dolores Hart, Prioress at the Abbey of Regina Laudis and former Paramount star. Joyce Duriga, my former OSV editor, now at *Catholic New World* in Chicago, loved the idea and published my piece soon thereafter.

Six months later, *Newport Life* published my Betty Hutton feature in its May 2009 "Best of Newport" issue. And I continued to pen pieces about other celebrities including John Wayne and Judy Garland on the thirtieth and fortieth anniversaries of their deaths, respectively, in *Big Hollywood*.

While these hard-won yet small publishing breaks were heartening, they were hardly enough. So I rekindled the idea of a book. It needed rekindling. By March 2010, after an unproductive screenwriting venture, I felt adrift. My friend, Michael Schwartz, Senator Tom Coburn's (R-OK) longtime chief of staff, gave me just the clarity I needed. "You're a good writer," he said, "and need to be writing books, not press releases and speeches." I just needed to decide what book, he said.

I knew the book.

After Patricia Neal died on August 8, 2010, I began reading her autobiography, *As I Am*—vowing to write about her in my book. However, by July 2011, after writing a piece for *National Catholic Register*, I decided to pitch my Cooper feature to the editor, Tom Wehner. He was interested and published my piece soon thereafter. I wrote three more pieces for the *Register* about Neal and Bob Hope and a combined feature about Wyman and Hutton.

In early 2012, I began writing my *Forbes* column, focused on Hollywood legends and celebrity recovery. Amazingly, all the conversion stories I began slipping into my submissions were steadily outpacing the others and rising to the top. I knew I had a book.

Michael, who, himself, had been diagnosed with Lou Gehrig's the summer of 2011, would suffer nearly two years, working almost to the end, until his death on February 4, 2013. A.C. became ill in May 2012 and died on September 27, 2013. Last but not least, my mother died unexpectedly on July 15, 2014. As bittersweet as their passings are, particularly in the case of my mother, all who read and profit by these stories are a testament to their legacy.

Acknowledgments

My deepest gratitude goes to my parents, Claire Yvonne and Paul Albert Kendall, married sixty years on April 24, 2014, without whose unconditional love and support this book, quite simply, would not exist. Heartfelt thanks, as well, goes to the late Michael Schwartz and A.C. Lyles for their gracious support and friendship throughout the years.

I also owe a special debt of gratitude to Maria Cooper Janis for sharing stories about her father and mother along with photos from the Gary Cooper Estate, for talking to me about Patricia Neal and for her warm friendship and support, telling me after my mother died, "Listen to her;" and to the late Fr. Benedict Groeschel, Cardinal Theodore McCarrick, and Fr. George Rutler for talking with me about Bob and Dolores Hope; Frs. Padraic Loftus, Mark Henninger, and Joseph Glynn and Howard Lincoln for sharing their stories of conversion about Ann Miller and Mary Astor, Alfred Hitchcock and Jane Wyman, respectively; Gretchen Wayne and A.J. Fenady for sharing stories about "the Duke;" Jane Withers for talking with me about Ann Miller; Marilyn Thorpe Roh for her reminiscences about her mother, Mary Astor; Joe Tracy for granting permission to include the never-before-published 1927 photo of his grandfather and father, Spencer and John; Harry Flynn, Bob Hope's former publicist, for his insights and stories; and Ewing Miles "Lucky" Brown, for his tales of Hollywood's "Golden Age;" among many others too numerous to name.

Special thanks, as well, goes to Frs. C. John McCloskey and Paul Grant for their warm friendship and sage advice; Tom Selz, for his expert counsel; Charles Scribner III, whose many "bravissimas" and other kudos in Italian and German—along with his expert advice—have warmed my heart and steadied my steps; the late Redd Griffin, a Hemingway scholar, who said my writing reminded him of "Papa" (Hemingway). If only!; Mark Metcalf, who told me after reading my Patricia Neal piece in *Forbes* that I was "a gigantic talent," impelling me to pursue a book publisher with greater urgency; Major General Jeffrey E. Phillips for writing me as I was starting to draft my book proposal, "Wow, I like your writing, Mary Claire. Tight and full of movement," albeit he later wondered about the wisdom of focusing on celebrities of yesteryear. Well, he can be forgiven, since he doesn't play heroes— he is one; and the late Dennis Helming, my writing collaborator on another book, who, after reading my revised proposal, wrote: "Wow!;" then, when my book was green-lighted, for his prescience in writing, "Congratulations and my condolences." (I did not know fully what he meant, but I do now!)

Finally, I am grateful to my editors on this book, particularly Katie Carroll and Mary Carol Kendzia, who are the tops.

Last but not least, I want to thank Mother Dolores Hart for writing the foreword from her privileged vantage point, providing insight into the power of these stories, and for talking with me about her "best friend" Patricia Neal, and being such a good friend to me, as well.

Introduction

Early on, when I was marketing Gary Cooper's faith journey, the editor of a Los Angeles-based magazine told me she was only interested in his "external life." How absurd, I thought. What can be more fascinating than the story of a soul? It's Billy Wilder's classic *Sunset Boulevard* (1950) about a silent movie queen, craving a return. It's *Barrymore* (2011) about Jack, youngest of the theatrical royal family, eying a comeback, in between sips. It's the arc of life, the ups and downs we all wrestle with, that completes the picture.

Herein are portraits of twelve Hollywood legends—Alfred Hitchcock, Gary Cooper, Bob Hope, Mary Astor, John Wayne, Ann Sothern, Jane Wyman, Susan Hayward, Lana Turner, Betty Hutton, Ann Miller, and Patricia Neal. And, while no one can know for certain the actual inner life of anyone, least of all a star, we do have certain clues—the most obvious being a religious conversion. You know something's going on when that happens. The trick is to try to understand the journey and all that led up to it. This requires careful study, peeling off the layers, one by one, like a good detective; then, like a good director, artfully choosing just the right scenes, moments, images to reveal character and motivations. What is fascinating is how the arc of each of their lives followed somewhat similar patterns and rhythms. But then, the human experience is unalterable. As Hemingway said, "Every man's life ends the same way, and it is only the details of how he lived and how he died that distinguishes one man from another."[1] Oh, but the details, as he well knew, are rich—details provided by interviews the stars gave; interviews with those who knew them best; their own writing—as with Astor, Turner, Hutton, Miller and Neal; and by their actions, chronicled by many dedicated biographers.

A word about Hollywood itself: It's a world that is particularly unique, and perhaps unparalleled, in creating the crisis of soul that can lead to conversion. The town, since its earliest days, has always had a rich tapestry of faiths for souls seeking spiritual sustenance, the respective houses of worship dotting the landscape, including Jewish, Roman Catholic, Orthodox (i.e., Russian, Greek, Eastern), Protestant—Episcopalian, Baptist, Presbyterian, Methodist, Lutheran, Congregational, Evangelical, and nondenominational, among others—as well as homegrown hybrids such as Mormon, Quaker, Unitarian Universalist, and the Church of Christ, Scientist, among others.

During Hollywood's Golden Age, a proportionately higher number of stars gravitated to the Catholic faith. The stories that follow reveal why.

So sit back and get ready to enjoy some of the best, most inspiring stories ever to come out of Hollywood. The rich and captivating world underlying them, I would argue, is more exciting than any computer-generated image in this century's digitally crafted films with action, action, action—leaving little room or time for the action of God, just below the surface.

Chapter One
• • •

ALL TOO HUMAN: THE NEED
FOR HEALING AND RECOVERY
• • •

The young man who rings the bell at the brothel is unconsciously looking for God.[1]

— Bruce Marshall

Betty Hutton told priests she met in Rhode Island in the 1970s, "Practically all the stars are in trouble. You happen to see me talking honestly to you. It's a nightmare out there! It hurts what we do in our private lives."[2]

It's a story as old as Hollywood itself. Stars, so talented in portraying human frailty, are, themselves, often all too human. Without a steady moral compass, fame and celebrity can lead to personal destruction. Hollywood has just the right siren calls to lead stars astray.

Originally founded as an oasis of health for the sickly in need of California's warm sunshine, salty air, and abundant fruits and vegetables, Hollywood would soon lure filmmakers, as well. Its flat expanses, favorable weather conditions, inexpensive labor, and freedom from Edison's trust enforcers, made it ideal for the nascent film industry.

D.W. Griffith, known as the "Father of Film," first captured Hollywood's landscape cinematically while shooting *Faithful* (1910) for the Biograph Company. Perhaps fittingly for Hollywood, the film had nothing to do with faith. Rather, it was about a tramp, named Faithful, who gets a second chance, only to ruin it by driving his benefactor nuts.

Mary Pickford was Griffith's big discovery. Born Gladys Smith in Toronto, Canada, in 1892, this golden-haired, English Irish beauty, had an uncanny ability to act for the camera and quickly went from the "Biograph girl" to "America's Sweetheart,"[3] becoming, as Jeanine Basinger writes in *Silent Stars*, "the 'first real star' in motion picture history."[4] She was also "the first woman in America to earn $1 million in one year."[5]

Mary was close to her mother, Charlotte Hennessey Smith, whose parents had migrated from County Kerry—"John Pickford Hennessey [bequeathing] to his children seductive Irish charm and a weakness for strong spirits."[6] He also bequeathed to them the Catholic faith. After Mary's father, John Charles Smith, died on February 11, 1898, Gladys, six, and Charlotte, twenty-four, forged a strong bond as they strove to survive. After six months at McCall School, Gladys took up acting to help support the family, including her two younger siblings "Lottie" and "Jack."

Charlotte was integral to her daughter's success and when she died of cancer in 1928, at age fifty-five, Mary sought solace from the parish priest, but found him cold. Into the void stepped The Church of Christ, Scientist, founded by Mary Eddy Baker forty-nine years earlier in Boston, ready with a warm embrace.

By the early twenties, the film industry had become the fifth largest U.S. business. At the same time, with the end of World War I, social mores were fast changing. Bucking this trend, in January 1920, the Volstead Act, banning the sale of intoxicating liquor, became the law of the land, ushering in F. Scott Fitzgerald's "Jazz Age" of speakeasies and flappers, with stars only too happy to play their leading role in this social revolution, abandoning

traditional moral constraints, when circumstances demanded—
even as the studio pressured them to be good.

Mary was no exception. She and Douglas
Fairbanks Sr. began seeing each other in
1916, while both were married to other
people. While divorce still carried a social
stigma, Mary got a swift Nevada divorce
and married Fairbanks on March 28, 1920.
Nevada contested it until 1922 as fans,
captivated by their storied lives, gave them
a moral pass. "Mary Pickford and Douglas
Fairbanks," writes Basinger, "represent the
birth of superstar celebrity; their success,

Mary Pickford

their talent, and their marriage to each other made them the first
King and Queen of Hollywood, and they have never been super-
seded."[7] But not everyone cheered their union.

Baptist Reverend J. Whitcomb Brougher, who married them,
was "openly rebuked for taking part in the ceremony."[8] And
Archbishop John J. Cantwell of the Catholic diocese of Monterey
and Los Angeles issued a statement on divorce, calling it "the
greatest of all modern evils."[9] Furthermore, Reverend Dr. John
Roach Straton denounced them from his New York City pulpit
for "demoralizing and corrupting the honorable institution of
marriage."[10] Doug was also at odds with his recently deceased
hero, Theodore Roosevelt, who considered marriage indissoluble.

Fairbanks loved Mary deeply, but jealousies arose when Buddy
Rogers, twenty-three, known for *Wings* (1928), began lavishing
attention on Mary, thirty-five, his costar in *My Best Girl* (1927).
In response, Doug began seeing spitfire Mexican actress Lupe
Velez. Add to the mix Charlotte's death and "talking" pictures,

displacing silent films, and Mary's calm was shattered. Seeking relief, Doug began seeing twenty-nine-year-old divorcee Lady Sylvia Ashley, and when the affair became public in 1933, Hollywood's royal couple split. That same year, Mary's baby brother, Jack—"Hollywood's favorite drunk"—died at age thirty-six; she made her last film, *Secrets* (1933); and prospects of reconciliation dimmed. When the couple divorced in 1936, Mary retained Pickfair, where she grieved the end of her marriage, the death of her cherished family members—now including her sister Lottie at age forty-three—and the demise of her career.

Mary turned to alcohol for consolation, and while she drank far less than her siblings, her condition underscored the sadness enveloping her life—including the sudden death of her beloved Doug on December 12, 1939, of a heart attack. Mary, whose first husband had died six months earlier, was now married to Rogers. But still deeply in love with Doug, she was heartbroken.

Yet, as tragic as the Pickford-Fairbanks saga was, worse scandals were hitting Hollywood.

One of the most sensational began unfolding over Labor Day weekend 1921, when popular comedian Roscoe "Fats" Arbuckle hosted a raucous party at San Francisco's St. Francis Hotel. It abruptly stopped when a little-known thirty-year-old actress named Virginia Rappe became ill and died three days later. Arbuckle, who had allegedly forced himself on her, was charged with manslaughter in her death and indicted, convulsing the industry. Though cleared on the third trial—a preexisting condition was deemed the cause of death—and acquitted with an apology from the jury, the damage to Arbuckle's career was complete. He died a broken man in 1933 at age forty-six.

In response to this and other scandals, Hollywood introduced a "morals clause" into actors' contracts, rendering agreements null and void if the actor was even suspected of, among other infractions, "adulterous conduct and immoral relations."[11]

Gloria Swanson was particularly vulnerable. Born in Chicago in 1899, of German, French, Polish, and Swedish descent, she arrived in Hollywood at age sixteen, having worked as a full-time actress in her hometown.

In contrast to Pickford's curls, Swanson sported a different hairstyle in every film, breaking taboos left and right. Seductive, modern, glamorous—women of America longed to be like her. But her questionable moral choices were nothing to emulate. First husband Wallace Beery, fourteen years her senior, "brutalized" the sixteen-year-old on their wedding night, "in pitchblackness" as he "whispered filth in my ear while he ripped me almost in two,"[12] she writes then slipped her "medicine" to abort their unborn child and spent her one-hundred-dollar weekly earnings from Keystone Studios on other women. She escaped to Triangle Pictures in Culver City, where Cecil B. DeMille soon discovered her, signing her to make six films capitalizing on the era's loosening mores, including *Don't Change Your Husband* (1919) *For Better, For Worse* (1919), *Male and Female* (1919) and *Something to Think About* (1920). Her name soon received top billing—above DeMille's.

By the time the morals clause went into effect, Swanson's affairs were well-known, including one with director Mickey Nielan, and to save her career, she had to pay her second husband, film distributor Herbert Sonborn, dearly. After divorcing him, she headed to France to film *Madame Sans-Gene* (1925) and began an affair with one Henri, a royal marquis. Discovering she was pregnant, she and Henri wed, and the next day she had an abortion, causing an infection that made her quite ill, though the true cause was shrouded: Food poisoning, it was alledged. After recovering, she made a triumphal return to the States, heralded as royalty.

Feeling sky-high, Swanson spurned the studio's unheard-of one-million-dollar offer for four pictures and, risking her career, headed to independent United Artists, at the suggestion of founders Pickford and Fairbanks, to make *Sadie Thompson* (1927). Fifteen members of the Motion Picture Producers and Distributors of America, including rising mogul Joseph P. Kennedy, found the story morally objectionable. She finessed it by changing the preacher, who is seduced, to a reformer. While she might be able to massage a storyline, she was no money manager. Worse, she was a spendaholic—a legacy of her days at Famous Players, where they clothed her in minks and diamonds and footed the bill for her correspondingly luxurious lifestyle off-screen, including five hundred dollars a month for perfume. After filming wrapped in the fall of 1927, deeply in debt, she turned to Kennedy to save her. He told her, "Together we could make millions," but refused to partner with her while she was saddled with debt.[13]

With her full approval, though not realizing how radical the financial surgery would need to be, Kennedy's henchmen proceeded stealthily to clean up her books, divest her of properties, pay her bills, clear her tax liability, get her released from her UA contract, and, finally, form a new production company, Gloria Productions—in a flash—of which Kennedy's aide, Pat Scollard, said, "If I don't go to jail on this deal, I never will."[14] Gloria Productions, for the next two years, became a pass-through for padded production costs at Pathé Studios, which Kennedy helmed—while getting sexual favors. In 1930, Kennedy abruptly resigned from Pathé and headed back East, leaving the former "reigning queen"[15] of Hollywood with regret over the baby she aborted during their affair and the millions he had fleeced her out of. When she played the aging silent film star in *Sunset Boulevard* in 1950, Pickford, seeing it, wept.

But not every star succumbed. Ethel Barrymore, great aunt of Drew Barrymore, was a refreshing contrast. Grand dame of the theatre and Oscar-winning actress, she hailed from two great theatrical families—the Drews and the Barrymores, going back to the seventeenth and eighteenth centuries, respectively.

And while she was given much grace, her life was also paved with sorrow.

She was born in Philadelphia, on August 15, 1879, some sixteen months after her brother, Lionel, and two and a half years before her brother John (a.k.a. Jack). Of her parents, Georgie and Maurice, both actors, she writes, "What a magic flame was lighted that Sunday in a small house in Philadelphia when they met." Not many Sundays elapsed before they were engaged and married—from which flowed Georgie's "command performances," i.e., the birth of her children in rapid succession.[16] In reward for Georgie's labors, "there came a magic day," she writes, when they took a "private train coach" to a theatre, where they were performing, and "the most charming and entrancing woman" entered their lives. For four-year-old Ethel, memories of the plays were vague, but, she writes, "Madam Modjeska was stamped on my mind and heart indelibly for my life, and my gratitude is unbounded." A "devout Catholic," her mother soon knew "she must be a Catholic, too. So suddenly Lionel and I were surprised to be baptized again." Jack, at home with Mummum (grandmother), "escaped for the time being."[17]

After that, her mother "was under the impression that she and Papa had something important in common—one of her incredibly few errors."[18]

When her mother became ill—"bronchitis they said," Ethel was suddenly yanked from the convent school to travel with her from New York to Santa Barbara, "where Mamma was to get well." The parting was "bad before the boat sailed" and "Mamma was saying good-bye to Papa and begging him not to forget her"— "my first sight of tragedy, although I didn't know it then," she writes.[19]

Her mother would die in California. The year was 1892. Ethel, just thirteen, was now the mother of the family and had John baptized. The same year, Mummum withdrew from the Arch Street Theatre she had managed since 1863 and moved into a boarding house, where she died on August 31, 1897. Ethel also had to deal with her increasingly erratic father, who, nine years after his wife's death, landed in an insane asylum, suffering from the effects of syphilis. He was dead four years later.

After burying her mother in Philadelphia, she briefly attended the Convent of the Sacred Heart in Philadelphia before entering the family trade to support herself—abandoning her dreams of becoming a pianist. She made her debut on January 25, 1894, in *The Rivals* at New York's now-defunct Empire Theatre, a Barrymore and Drew theatrical home. But her famous name proved more hindrance than help—"Nothing today!" persistently greeted her—until her Uncle John Drew stepped in to find Ethel a bit part in *The Bauble Shop* (1894), produced by Charles Froman. After several years of such small roles, touring the country on a shoestring, she steadily grew on audiences and impressed critics. When Frohman cast her in the role of Mme. Trentoni in *Captain*

Jinks of the High Horse Marines, she rocketed to stardom.

Soon internationally known, she wore a distinctive hairstyle, widely imitated, along with her walk and talk. While living most summers abroad, she gathered a who's who of friends—presidents, prime ministers, kings, queens, and nobility by birth and accomplishment. Meeting all this royalty, she writes, was nothing new. She had, after all, known her grandmother.

Among her friends were many suitors, including two temporary fiancés. But when she met Russell Griswold Colt, three years her junior, convinced he was the one, they became engaged and married six months later on March 14, 1909, in Boston while *Lady Frederick* was playing.

"I went to see Bishop O'Connell," she writes, "to arrange for a dispensation to marry a Protestant." The bishop—later a cardinal—completely fascinated Russell when he stopped by to sign the necessary documents.

"That's the most charming man I have ever met," he said, asking, "How do you get to be a Catholic?' But, he never did anything about it," she writes.[20]

The couple wed on a Sunday morning at the priest's house at the Church of the Most Precious Blood in Hyde Park. After their baby Samuel Peabody Colt—"Sammy"—was born on November 28, 1909, Ethel continued acting, while keeping a careful watch on her baby, installing a phone in her dressing room—perhaps the first time a phone was installed in a dressing room and "certainly the first for such a reason."[21] But while her mothering was smooth, her marriage was rocky.

Russell's father, Colonel Pomeroy Colt, had warned Ethel about her son's lack of financial stability. "I don't want money," Ethel replied. She liked his "tremendous humour." Colonel Colt bought them a house in Mamaroneck, while Russell continued tripping into his job at Horton and Company each day. (Asked what train he took into work, he said, "I usually miss the 10:37."[22]) By summer 1911, the reality of Russell's breezy irresponsibility settled in, and Ethel filed for a divorce, only to change her mind, making possible the birth of her two other children, Ethel Barrymore Colt and John Drew "Jackie" Colt, on April 30, 1912, and September 9, 1913, respectively.

After her daughter was born, Ethel landed a role in *The Twelve Pound Look*, playing the Orpheum Circuit "all over the West" for three thousand dollars a week, in what would be a recurring role. "Then I wrote to Mr. Frohman and asked why I couldn't play all over the East." So she did—for a year and "twice broke the Palace Theatre record."[23]

Ten days after Jackie was born, Ethel was back on the Empire stage, rehearsing for *Tante*.

Russell, after discovering he had bronchitis, she writes, soon decided he would need to spend the winters in Palm Beach and, lucky for him, there was a branch office there!

In spite of the marital tensions, there were happy times, she writes, especially given their mutual interest in sports. Yet, for all they shared—not least of which three beautiful children—she could not ignore his infidelity, and the couple divorced in 1923, Ethel promising the cardinal she would not remarry—which she found somewhat amusing. She had no intention of remarrying, given all she endured.

Her theatrical career would continue, which, more than a hindrance to her marriage, she writes, had made it as strong and resilient for as long as it was. The couple remained friends, with Sam visiting on holidays.

Her days on stage included the exhilarating experience in 1919 of being able to support her fellow actors striking against a changing theatre in which actors were mere pawns in making money. In contrast, she had experienced producers like Froman—sadly a casualty of the *Lusitania*'s sinking—who had treated players with utmost respect.

She also witnessed with delight her brother John's Broadway triumphs—following his silent screen stardom—including, at his zenith, *Hamlet* in 1925, after which he slowly descended into alcoholism until a heart attack claimed his life on May 29, 1942.

In 1944, after half a century on the stage, she retired from theater and began focusing on film, TV, and radio, including her Oscar-winning role in *None but the Lonely Heart* (1944). Finally, after some blessed years in Palos Verdes, she settled in Beverly Hills, in a humble abode she lived in with her son, Sammy, who helped her navigate her final years.

She used her talent to spread the Gospel as well, reading the Passion story from St. Matthew for Father Peyton's *Family Theatre* on Easter. The effect was profound. Protestants as well as Catholics sent in thousands of letters "including one that deeply touched me from M.A. De Wolfe Howe," who said, she writes, "although he had thought he had been hearing St. Matthew all his life, he had never really heard him before."[24]

A mark of her saintliness is revealed by her recollection late in life that "I have never been able to bear malice toward anybody, although there have been plenty of opportunities for it." Rather she preferred to remember the good times. "The best of all," she writes, was the birthday party The Academy of Motion Picture Arts and Sciences hosted for her seventieth birthday celebration.[25] Spencer Tracy, speaking of his Broadway experience with her in

The Royal Fandango (1924), recalled, "You, Miss Barrymore, were the star. I had one line. On the opening night I stood waiting for my entrance, shakily wondering whom they'd get to replace me the second night. Suddenly you stopped beside me and said quietly, 'Relax. That's all you have to do—just relax.'... I've been capitalizing on that advice ever since."[26]

Five years after this glowing night, a bright star in her life would dim when she lost her other beloved brother, Lionel—like John, the victim of a heart attack—on November 15, 1954. She died in Hollywood, California, on June 18, 1959, six months after her husband.

Ethel Barrymore was, of course, the exception, her brother John more the rule in terms of Hollywood celebrities, often less than exemplary behavior. To be sure, she had plenty of help, including Sister Julie de St. Esprit, the memory of whose admonishment—"Really, Ethel, don't be absurd!"—was sufficient to steer her away from trouble.[27]

Similarly, Spencer Tracy had good Jesuit priests guiding him. But he was uniquely complex, his father playing a huge role in his life. As his brother, Carroll, said, "Dad was a tough, decisive, no-nonsense man, and there was never any doubt that we'd be raised as Catholics. When we were old enough, Spence and I both became altar boys.... One of dad's greatest hopes was that one of us would become a priest."[28]

Ethel Barrymore's advice was profound. She must have had an intuitive feel for him. "Relax, just relax," was just the salve his soul needed. As a teen, in fact, Tracy felt called to be a priest or possibly a doctor. But he did not have the grades for Latin—or chemistry, for that matter—and, more importantly, had the passion to act.[29] As he later jokingly recalled, "I wouldn't have gone to school at all if there'd been any other way to read the subtitles in films."[30]

His peers considered this two-time Oscar-winner Hollywood's greatest actor. He also sometimes acted like Hollywood's greatest sinner. The essence of this complex man was the guilt he felt—not understanding or accepting, given his tense, exacting nature, that God gave him the soul of an actor, not a priest. Then, too, there was the loneliness, which his friend, Garson Kanin, believed was the "single wellspring" of his tortured psyche and his genius.[31] In God's plan, his angst infused his work with unmatched brilliance, while off-camera he grappled with that distorted image of God as stern judge. Life, he once said, was something he was not very good at. But an honest tally—not the severe accounting his brooding Irish nature concocted—shows, with no little irony, a man with great generosity of spirit, the wellspring of which is divine love, Tracy's image of a stern God, notwithstanding.

Toward the end of his life, after suffering misplaced guilt over his son, John, whose disability he felt in some way responsible for—that and other sources of guilt, e.g., not becoming the priest his father wanted, only acting one—he began rereading the great classics of Catholic literature he had devoured as a teen, as he ailed with heart disease. Then, too, he reconnected with Msgr. John O'Donnell, the technical advisor on *Boys Town* (1938).

He died on June 10, 1967, just after finishing *Guess Who's Coming to Dinner* (1967). The funeral Mass, was held at the Immaculate Heart of Mary Church in Hollywood, celebrated by Monsignor O'Donnell. Tracy had done his life's work, moving souls, telling the truth, through his craft. Now, he was ready to go back to God.

Many stars, though, succumb, whether because they lack a clear moral compass or lack the strength to follow it. Just ask Carol

Landis, Margaret Sullavan, Marilyn Monroe, Barbara Payton, Judy Garland, or Florence Lawrence, the first Biograph star in the early 1900s before Pickford eclipsed her in 1909. She committed suicide in 1938 by eating ant paste. As for Sullavan, Jimmy Stewart's costar in Ernst Lubitsch's classic, *The Shop Around the Corner* (1940), she telegraphed in a final interview, shortly before her death by barbiturate overdose on New Year's Day 1960 at age fifty, "I loathe what [acting] does to my life. It cancels it out."[32] She wanted to spend more time with her children.

Fast-forward some fifty years, and the cruel nightmare lives on. Lindsay Lohan, Mel Gibson, Robert Downey Jr., Charlie Sheen, and so many others have trod Hollywood's well-worn chemically induced path to meltdown—many including Peaches Geldorf, Philip Seymour Hoffman, Lisa Robin Kelly, Cory Monteith, Whitney Houston, Amy Winehouse, Heath Ledger, Chris Penn, Chris Farley, River Phoenix, John Belushi, and Elvis Presley, among many others, losing their battle to drugs and dying much too young.

Recovery is often as much, if not more, a matter of the soul as of the body.

Many stars, so skilled at listening, finally hear the voice of God, and, having experienced the dark side of Hollywood, recover with the light of faith. That so many have found faith is only natural, given how in tune they are with their feelings. Faith, when it is real, builds on what is most human in us. As Pope St. John Paul II, himself an actor and playwright in his youth, said in Washington, D.C., in October 1979: "When you find Christ, you find your humanity."[33]

What follows are twelve stories of legendary stars who found their humanity by knocking on the right door—in some cases, at the end of a very long road.

Chapter Two
• • •

ALFRED HITCHCOCK COMES
FULL CIRCLE
• • •

Fear? It has influenced my life and
my career.[1]

— ALFRED HITCHCOCK

In 1980, as Sir Alfred Hitchcock
confronted his mortality, he reached out to his old friend Fr.
Thomas James Sullivan for spiritual strength and solace. Sullivan,
who was "a priest to the stars,"[2] brought along a young priest by
the name of Fr. Mark Henninger that first Saturday. They visited
"Hitch" several more times over the course of the next year or
so—always on Saturday.

One Saturday, Fr. Henninger came alone. After chatting for a
while in his living room, Hitch said, "Come, let's have mass."[3]
As Fr. Henninger began to help the ailing director along the
breezeway of his Bel Air home,[4] step by agonizing step, Hitch
remained silent, prompting the tongue-tied priest to blurt out,
"Have you seen any good movies, Mr. Hitchcock?"[5]

"When I made movies they were about people, not robots,"
Hitchcock replied emphatically after an initial pause. "Robots are
boring. Come on, let's have Mass."[6]

Sixty years earlier, Hitchcock's eagerness for making films had
trumped all. Now, with the Reagan era dawning and his health
failing, the legendary director was focused on the greatest drama
of all—that of Christ's pure love and healing forgiveness.

Unique among the twelve Hollywood legends profiled herein, the famed director was raised in a devout, if irreverent, Catholic family. He was not an actor but worked mostly behind the camera, though he was known for his iconic cameos and his television program *Alfred Hitchcock Presents*. But, like all the legends herein, as he ascended the Hollywood ladder, God increasingly became an afterthought. The same care his parents put into cultivating his faith, he put into cultivating his films. And, while his wife, fellow director Alma Reville, converted to Catholicism in the wake of their 1926 nuptials, it failed to stick, Hitchcock wrote in a private letter, and he drifted away along with her.[7] Now, half a century later, while eating little, he felt a deep thirst for God. What this man, so utterly fascinated with all manner of human darkness and depravity, needed most, it turned out, was God's light and grace.

A Close-Knit English Catholic family

Alfred Joseph Hitchcock was born in Leytonstone, England, northeast of London, on August 13, 1899, to William and Emma Jane (nee Whelan) Hitchcock—the youngest of three, including William and Nellie, born in 1890 and 1892, respectively. Since mid-century, Leytonstone had mushroomed. Formerly the province of wealthy merchants with grand rural estates, it was now dotted with inexpensive dwellings for city workers, boasting a bustling commercial center with shops, churches, and schools.

His father, one of six children, was a greengrocer, continuing the family business, though his youngest brother, John, was there to help his hard-drinking brother in a pinch. His mother, the daughter of a policeman, "was second-generation Irish, Catholic, literate," with black-Irish humor. One year William's junior, Emma "was very sensible and likely kept the books for her husband."[8]

Contrary to the image perpetuated, Hitchcock, "was part of a large, loving family, with whom he remained close throughout his life"—making sure to visit relatives when filming in a nearby location.[9]

The Catholic faith pervaded family life. His father's sister, Emma, Hitch's favorite aunt, traveled by rickshaw to Mass all her life, after she moved to South Africa to marry.[10] His mother required him to recite his "evening confession" at day's end, complemented by weekly confession and Mass on Sundays at a parish in Stratford, where his father's nephew, Fr. John, ministered.

After Sunday Mass, William Hitchcock would treat his children to picnics in Epping Forest and often took them to shows at the nearby Borough Theater, which infused Hitch early on with a love for theatre. Home was often theater enough. At frequent gatherings various family members, including some real characters, shared the latest gossip or grisly murder, revealing human nature at its most complex—Jack the Ripper having done his killing in nearby Whitechapel. At these get-togethers, Hitchcock's more reflective style came through. As he said years later, "I would sit quietly in a corner, saying nothing. I looked and observed a good deal. I've always been that way."[11]

The virtue his parents and teachers inculcated in him also shined through. As authorized biographer John Russell Taylor writes, "He did not go to parties, he did not have affairs with glamour stars, he did not really do anything but make pictures."[12]

When he was six, his family moved down the Lea River to Salmon Lane, Limehouse, in Stepney borough, to take over two fish stores, at 130 and 175 Salmon Lane, part of the burgeoning business John Hitchcock Ltd. was developing—peaking at sixty-nine London shops in 1925. "The boy's formative years, roughly from 1907 to 1915 were lived in the shadow of warehouses and wharves and the muddy, smelly Thames."[13] A neighborhood not unlike that in *Marnie* (1964), filmed after the trio that cemented his reputation—*North by Northwest* (1959), *Psycho* (1960) and *The Birds* (1963).

The Jesuit training he received at St. Ignatius College, starting in the fall of 1910, particularly instilled in him the discipline to succeed, given what he called "Jesuit reasoning power," "a strong sense of fear," and grounding in reality. "These were the cornerstones of his art. No director was more disciplined, more ordered in his thinking."[14] Besides a full complement of sports, academics, arts, and literature, St. Ignatius had a rigorous spiritual program including Mass at 8:45 A.M. before classes, daily catechism lessons, optional Friday confession, plus a required annual three-day retreat. The school also instilled in him a sense of drama. As Fr. Henninger said, St. Ignatius "had a Master of Discipline, so if any of the boys misbehaved during the day...the Master of Discipline" would deal with him—at days end, leaving you in suspense all day, "wondering what he's going to do to you."[15] Out of that experience was born the "Master of Suspense."

Engineering and Film

Leaving school shortly after his father's death in 1914, Hitchcock landed work at the W.T. Henley Telegraph Company, an electrical cable manufacturer and installer. In contrast to his experience at St. Ignatius, he was well-liked at Henley and even managed to sport a trim figure at times.

While continuing his work at Henley during World War I, by 1917, militarily ranked C3, and only suitable for sedentary work, he finally joined the Royal Engineers volunteer corps. He learned how to lay charges and "once took part in practical exercises in

Hyde Park," writes Taylor, but "could never get his puttees wound properly and they kept falling round his ankles."[16] He enrolled in art courses at Goldsmith's College, which heightened his interest in theater and soon film, in which he came to appreciate America's "technical superiority."[17] At Henley, it had become apparent he was not suited for administrative work either—he let his paper-work pile up until motivated to zoom through it—and he was transferred to sales, and then advertising, where he flourished. He wrote short stories for publication in *The Telegraph*, starting in June 1919. And as his love of cinema grew, he scouted out the London studios. In late 1920, he read that British Famous Players-Lasky was opening a London branch. After some aggres-sive courting, he left Henley on April 27, 1921, to take charge of the art title department at their Islington studio. But the venture was suspended in summer 1922—two new studios in Long Island and London proving financially unstable—but not before Hitch spotted his future wife, Alma Reville, then an assistant director. He said nothing, such silence being strategic, but watched and waited, until he was a director, she no longer at Islington. Part of a skeleton crew, he was on his way up. "Working longer hours for less money, he thrived."[18] And thrived—especially with the help of Alma, whom he married on December 2, 1926.

He had struggled in the intervening years, hitting his stride with *The Lodger: A Story of the London Fog*, a suspense film premised on the hot pursuit of a Jack-the-Ripper-type serial killer. Released in January 1927 to great commercial success and critical acclaim, it is considered the first "Hitchcockian" film, complete with the "wrong man" theme.

From there, he rocketed to the top, becoming England's premier director, with such films as *The 39 Steps* (1935), *Secret Agent*

(1936), *The Lady Vanishes* (1938), and *Jamaica Inn* (1939)—before being lured to America by David O. Selznick, where, out of the chute, he made Oscar-winning *Rebecca* (1940), then *Foreign Correspondent* (1940) and other war-themed films, as he worked to lure America to Britain's cause. But his greatest motivation was to make good films. As Hitchcock said, "The only thing I know how to do is make movies. I could never retire—what else is there?"[19]

Beyond Film—to Eternity

Hitch finally did retire, after making his fifty-fourth and last film, *The Family Plot* (1976). His body had begun to break down, and his soul to awaken.

In August 1979, shortly after he turned eighty, Ingrid Bergman visited him. "He took both my hands," she said, "and tears streamed down his face and he said, 'Ingrid, I'm going to die.'" She helped him by telling him, "Of course." We're all going to die, she said, telling him of her recent illness. "And for a moment, the logic of that seemed to make him more peaceful," she said.[20]

Then, too, there was the logic of his faith.

Shortly after that meeting with Bergman, he called Fr. Sullivan to say he wanted to go to confession. Or, as Fr. Sullivan characterized it, "He wants to come back home, back to the church." "I'm going over there Friday to hear confession," Fr. Sullivan told Fr. Henninger, "and if you want to come over Saturday, we'll have Mass in his little home."[21]

Hitchcock had met Fr. Sullivan while filming *The Paradine Case* (1947) and they had stayed in touch since then. Sullivan lived at Catholic Marymount College (later Loyola Marymount) and was close to Henninger, then a philosophy student at UCLA, living at the same residence.

Hitchcock had not exactly left the Church. He was a generous donor, publicly giving twenty thousand dollars to his alma mater, St. Ignatius, for a new chapel, and privately serving as a benefactor for churches and chapels throughout California.[22] And, according to his granddaughter, Fr. Henninger said, he was always a "good Catholic," ensuring the grandchildren got to Mass on Sundays when their parents—their mother, Patricia, who was the Hitchcocks' only child, and their father, Joseph Edward O'Connell—went on trips, leaving them with the grandparents.

"Hitchcock didn't drive," Fr. Henninger said, as told to him by the granddaughter. "So they had the chauffeur take them over. But one Sunday, there was no chauffer. So Hitchcock got behind the wheel and drove them to church. And, she said it was scary. So, give credit to Hitchcock," said Henninger.

When they came that first Saturday for Mass, Alma joined her husband. But, Henninger said, that was the only time. Henninger surmises that just as Hitch had come to appreciate and love his wife more fully later in life, as portrayed in the film *Hitchcock* (2012), he now savored his faith, realizing what comfort and clarity it provided.

"After we chatted for a while, we all crossed from the living room through a breezeway to his study, and there, with his wife, Alma, we celebrated a quiet Mass. Across from me were the bound volumes of his movie scripts, *The Birds*, *Psycho*, *North by Northwest* and others—a great distraction.... Hitchcock had been away from the church for some time, and he answered the responses in Latin the old way. But the most remarkable sight was that after receiving communion, he silently cried, tears rolling down his huge cheeks."[23]

Hitchcock died on April 29, 1981. He was buried from Good Shepherd Church in Beverly Hills. In his eulogy, Fr. Sullivan said, "We hope that Hitch rests in peace." Then, he caught himself. "No let's take that back. Not peace. Life. That's what Hitchcock loved. And, that's what we wish for him."[24]

Chapter Three

• • •

GARY COOPER'S QUIET JOURNEY OF FAITH

• • •

He was a poet of the real. He knew all about cows, bulls, cars, and ocean tides. He had the enthusiasm of a boy. He could always tell you his first vivid impression of a thing. He had an old-fashioned politeness, but he said nothing casually.[1]
— CLIFFORD ODETS, PLAYWRIGHT AND DRAMATIST, ON GARY COOPER

Hollywood icon Gary Cooper, known for such classics as *Mr. Deeds Goes to Town* (1936), *Sergeant York* (1941), *The Pride of the Yankees* (1942), and *High Noon* (1952), understood, to his core, the art of acting as few actors have. His formula was simple yet subtle, his talent and resonance undeniable. He single-handedly revived Paramount Pictures's sagging Depression-era fortunes and, at the pinnacle of his career, was the highest-paid American.[2]

Yet, this low-key, it's-*not*-all-about-me American original loved nothing more than to retreat from the bright lights to be one with nature on the vast plains or against the roaring ocean—to luxuriate in, listen to, observe and paint these natural settings, with family or friends, if not alone. He was an avid hunter and fisher, who loved subduing wild game and piscatorial poundage, and wearing signature garb of his Native American friends from childhood, including feather-bedecked war bonnets and moccasins, which he made himself.

He was a loyal friend, with a range of intimates including Ernest Hemingway and Jimmy Stewart, his closest friend. But more than anything, he was a devoted husband and father.

This, and so much more, defined "Coop," as his friends and peers called him. Then, after years of suffering personal turmoil, realizing that his strengths often became weaknesses, he began opening himself up to the truest friend of all and, in the process, had a spiritual conversion.

It was the most consequential subplot in his life's journey. But, contrary to frequent reports asserting otherwise, his embrace of religion was not prompted by illness. "No way," his daughter Maria Cooper Janis said. "He was coming to this on his own, in his own time…bits and pieces of his own life that he wanted to put together in a new way."[3]

It was a logical progression. "He had a very real spirituality," Maria said, "that wasn't an 'ism'…that, I think, he was born with, that he grew up with, living out West in nature (and) having a very strong affinity for the American Indian culture and spirituality."[4]

Groomed for Hollywood — Old West and English Manners
Born in Helena, Montana on May 7, 1901, as the Old West was fading, Cooper was an accidental star.

Around the time he was fifteen, while driving to Wesleyan with a friend, who was disabled by polio, the car's brakes failed. After hurtling down the steep mountain incline, the car stopped and jackknifed, falling on Cooper. In severe pain for months, unaware he had broken his hip, he continued riding his horse—learning to anticipate the horse's hard gallop; and, failing to heal properly, he acquired that distinctive Cooper walk. As he convalesced, he had time to reflect and study, which cemented in him the desire to become a commercial artist.

After graduating from Grinnell College in Iowa, he moved to Hollywood, arriving on Thanksgiving Day 1924, at his parents' new home in that oasis of health. However, commercial art jobs were scarce, so he landed stunt work instead and was soon "discovered." In 1925, he began acting in uncredited roles.

His film career, spanning thirty-six years, took off with *Wings* (1927), the first Best Picture Oscar-winner. His scene was a short one—just two-and-a-half minutes long. But, as Paramount Pictures legend A.C. Lyles said, "When he came on the screen, it just lit up with him."[5] With only two hundred feet of film, Hollywood moguls knew they were looking at a star.

Indeed, they were.

Cooper embodied American goodness and strength, projecting it on the screen with understated brilliance. His upbringing— raised Anglican in the Old West by English immigrant parents, who inculcated in him the manners of a "gentleman"—nurtured in him that unique American combination of rugged individualism and magnanimous selflessness.

"With Gary, there are always wonderful hidden depths that you haven't found yet," *Mr. Deeds Goes to Town* costar Jean Arthur said. "You feel like you're resting on the Rock of Gibraltar."[6]

Cooper was most closely identified with the Western, having starred in *The Virginian* (1929), the original, standard-setting film of that genre, where good always triumphed over evil. *High Noon* (1952), his second Oscar-winning film, often considered his greatest, revealed the moral struggle in this victory.

"I like Westerns because the good ones are real," Cooper said in a 1959 interview. "You feel real when you make them…[and]

realize that our country was and is full of people who believe in America."[7]

"He always said he wanted to make films that showed the best a man could be," Maria said. And there was no one like Coop to rise to those heights. As screenwriter and director Richard Brooks said, Cooper was a "great movie actor" because "he can make you feel something, something visceral, something deep, something that matters. He *is* who he plays."[8]

Quiet Masculinity and Piercing Blue Eyes

His cinematic choices perfectly complemented his personal traits. At the same time, he had a tragic flaw, exploited by the theatrical world, which laid traps for this elegantly handsome man, whose quiet masculinity and piercing blue eyes made him ready prey for legions of women desiring his companionship.

After some colorful romances with his costars, including "It Girl" Clara Bow (*Children of Divorce*, 1927)—along with Lupe Velez (*The Wolf Song*, 1929), Marlene Dietrich (*Morocco*, 1930), Carole Lombard (*I Take This Woman*, 1931) and Tallulah Bankhead (*Devil and the Deep*, 1932)—Cooper took time off in 1931–1932 to recuperate from the stresses of filmmaking, if not his whirlwind romancing. Hollywood had made great demands on its new star, who was ringing up the cash registers as the publicity machine cranked up the romances.

It all added up to a nervous breakdown for Coop. As he wrote his nephew Howard: "I had drifted, taken advice, let people get at me through my emotions, my sympathy, my affections."[9] For solace and healing, he gravitated to Europe, given his fond childhood memories of living in England some twenty years earlier. During his time away, he began to get a taste of high society as the guest of the Italian Countess Carla Dentice di Frasso.

Settling Down—Sort Of

Back in Hollywood by April 1932, feeling fully rejuvenated, he was soon introduced to the lovely New York socialite Veronica "Rocky" Balfe, who was visiting her uncle, Cedric Gibbons, MGM's art director, and his wife, Mexican actress Dolores del Rio. Twelve years his junior, Rocky was Catholic and had refined manners, which some detractors called Eastern snobbery. But Coop loved her—and her stabilizing and calming influence was just what he needed. They wed on December 15, 1933.

The Coopers were a gorgeous couple and bonded well, doing everything together, especially sports—hunting, horseback riding, canoeing, skeet shooting, tennis, biking—and raising Sealeyham pups, before their baby girl, Maria, came along on September 15, 1937.

Of their daughter, Maria—their only child, married to world-renowned classical pianist Byron Janis—Cooper said, "I've never known her to do anything that wasn't right. She is my life."[10]

"Ours was a unique family togetherness that was obvious and operative," Maria writes. It included "family traditions" such as the "Sunday swim in the ocean after Mass," which Rocky and she attended wearing bathing suits under their clothes. Afterward, Maria writes, "we'd zip up the street to our house in Brentwood, get Poppa, who had been studying or working in his gun room or catching forty more winks, pile the dogs in the car, and take off for Santa Monica."[11] "I could always see the love between my parents," Maria writes.[12]

But the marriage began to hit some turbulence in the summer of 1943, when gossip columns reported Cooper was keeping company with his *For Whom the Bell Tolls* (1943) costar Ingrid

Bergman. By 1946–1947, Hollywood and its legion of fawning women had become unbearable for Rocky.

As Richard Widmark summed it up, Cooper was "catnip to the ladies."[13] From the start, his affairs with leading ladies were always brief—going with the filmmaking territory, where falling in love on screen simply continued off screen.

A Complicated Situation

The affair with Patricia Neal was different. The two costarred in *The Fountainhead* (1949) and only became romantic after filming wrapped in October 1948. By Christmas 1951, Cooper saw how the affair was affecting his family and his health. So he gave Neal, twenty-five years his junior, a fur coat and left for Europe—exactly a year after he had taken her to Cuba, seeking his friend Hemingway's approval, which he failed to get.

This situation was difficult on everyone involved. Cooper suffered debilitating ulcers, and his family, along with Neal, endured intense emotional strain, complicated by Neal's pregnancy, which, to her later regret, she terminated.

But God brought good out of evil. After separating from his

family in May 1951, Coop came to see the emptiness in his life. "While he enjoyed his bachelor life," Maria writes, "my father realized this was not really making him happy."[14] His character Will Kane in *High Noon*, filmed in the fall of 1951, reflected perfectly the moral conflict he was feeling.

Gary Cooper meeting Pope Pius XII

Just as he was coming to terms with his own deeper needs, the family traveled to Europe in June 1953 for a *High Noon* publicity tour, which included a visit to the Vatican. (Though separated, they continued visiting and traveling together, and Coop stayed in touch with letters and phone calls.) On June 26, they met Pope Pius XII, which made a lasting impression on Cooper, still "years away from becoming a Catholic."[15] Like the awkwardly shy and endearing everyman characters he played in his films, his real-life persona infused this dramatic moment with some classic ordinariness.

Everyone in Hollywood was begging for a memento. So at the papal audience, Maria said, "my father had rosaries up his arm" in addition to the other mementos he was holding. But because of his bad back, he had trouble genuflecting and, as he did, "everything just fell—the medals, and the rosaries and the holy cards." They all went rolling across the floor, and carpet, into other guests' shoes, even under the Pontiff's robes. While Cooper was scrambling on all fours "suddenly," she said, he encountered "this scarlet shoe and a robe." And, as she writes, "There was the American actor Gary Cooper groping around in monumental embarrassment...with Pius XII looking down and patiently smiling."[16]

While in Italy, the family also visited their foster child, Raffaela Gravina, who lived in a small mountainside town outside of Naples, impoverished during the war from relentless bombing. The Coopers funded Raffaela's education and basic necessities and that of her remaining family. "VIVA GARY COOPER, VIVA GARY COOPER," written in white paint on the dirt road, expressed the town's gratitude. "They crowded around us," writes Maria, "and I saw such a look of compassion on my father's face, it made me want to cry."[17]

In February 1954, when Maria was sixteen, her father returned home just as he finished filming *Return to Paradise* (1953), about a father who returns home to love and nurture his sixteen-year-old daughter.

He missed his "dear girls" while he was oceans away, filming on location. Moreover, Rocky had "found her own self" in those years of separation. She socialized, gained a reputation as a fabulous host and, "impressed my father," Maria writes, "with her own glamour, spunk, and verve"—exactly the elements that "were important for him in a woman."[18]

After settling back into married life, he strayed again at times, gallingly going for less-refined women—his affair with the Swedish actress Anita Ekberg a salient example. "It seemed like a good idea at the time,"[19] he sheepishly told his wife with that classic boyish innocence. She wasn't amused.

Settling Down — for Good

After Sunday Mass together, Maria said, they would joke about "the very erudite, funny" Fr. Harold Ford—"a real man," whom her father called "Father Tough Stuff." Cooper was intrigued by what he had to say, and said, "Oh, I'd like to hear him some day." So Rocky said, "Well, come along." So he did—this time, outside the ordinary Christmas and Easter routine.

Though he never talked about it, Maria senses that, after her father returned home, "he probably was looking for some more stability than he found personally...." Father Ford's sermons made him think, she said. Everything was coming together.

"I know he realized in the last five years of his life," said Maria, "with incredible gratitude all the blessings he'd been given," and he wanted to "acknowledge it externally.... And, I think having a living, active connection to a spiritual structure, which he had never had...was part of the appeal." And, so, some fifteen years after making *Sergeant York*—Cooper's favorite and most memorable role, for which he won his first Oscar—he was walking in York's footsteps, spiritually.

Contrary to some accounts, Rocky did not engineer her husband's conversion. "It wasn't knocking him over the head," Maria said. "Because, believe me, no one made my father do what he didn't want to do." However, she did invite Fr. Ford to their home, thinking the two men might share some spiritual reflections. Instead they shared their mutual interest in guns, hunting, fishing and scuba diving. "Father Ford," writes Maria, "became a scuba buddy and joined us diving in the large marine land of the Pacific tank where we all cavorted with its inhabitants."[20]

"A little religion wouldn't do him no hurt"

In the midst of cavorting, the talk occasionally began to drift toward religion. As Alvin York, said, "A fellow can't go looking for it; it's just got to come to a fellow." Fr. Ford and Cooper began getting together for longer discussions about faith on drives up to Malibu and elsewhere. Gradually, Cooper evidently concluded, in Ma York's famous words, "a little religion wouldn't do him no hurt" and, in fact, could do him good. As he told Hollywood reporter Ruth Waterbury:

> Last winter, when I began trying to find out how to be less of a bum, I saw that religion is a sort of check up on yourself, a kind of patterned way of behaving. As I saw it, if a fellow goes to church, any church, and tries to straighten out his mind, it sure helps. After I digested that idea, I began thinking how our family had always done everything together.... Therefore, I figured if I was trying to change from the careless sloppy sort of guy I am, it seemed silly to go to a different church from the one my girls attend."[21]

On April 9, 1959, Gary Cooper was formally admitted into the Catholic Church. Close family friend Shirley Burden, himself a convert, served as Cooper's godfather at his baptism, and Dolores Hart was his godmother. Burden—Cornelius Vanderbilt's great-great-grandson, whose wife was Douglas Fairbanks Sr.'s niece—met with Cooper several times beforehand to help him understand this role of a lifetime. He knew it would not be easy, as Cooper reflected in the same interview with Waterbury shortly after his conversion:

> I'd spent all my waking hours…doing almost exactly what I, personally, wanted to do and what I wanted to do wasn't always the most polite thing either.… This past winter I began to dwell a little more on what's been in my mind for a long time (and thought), "Coop, old boy, you owe somebody something for all your good fortune." I guess that's what started me thinking seriously about my religion. I'll never be anything like a saint. I know. I just haven't got that kind of fortitude. The only thing I can say for me is that I'm trying to be a little better. Maybe I'll succeed.[22]

Putting Faith to the Test

On April 14, 1960, five months after Cooper visited Russia with his family and a Hollywood entourage, he had surgery for prostate cancer.[23] While the doctors deemed the operation successful, by May 31, the symptoms had returned and doctors again operated to remove a malignant tumor from his large intestine, this time confident he was cancer-free. On December 27, however, Rocky was informed the cancer had spread to Coop's lungs and bones. While she kept this heartbreaking news from her husband until February, he must have sensed the end was near. While filming *The Naked Edge* (1961) in London—the only film he made in his parents' native England—he had severe pain in his neck and shoulders and needed to take frequent oxygen breaks.

In December 1960, back in the States, Cooper filmed his last project—a TV program called "The Real West," which Maria said, "reflects my father's great love of the West"—the real West.[24] In March, he flew to New York to record the off-camera narration. TV producer Donald Hyatt recalled Cooper's "simplicity and lack of 'big star' pretentions," evident by his reaction when there was no room for his coat on the rack. "Don't take another coat off," Cooper said. "Just throw mine anywhere."[25]

In February and March of 1961, he continued entertaining friends. But by April, his condition began deteriorating. Saturday, April 15, would be the last time he ventured out—on the occasion of the remarriage of director Fred Zinneman to his wife of twenty-six years, Rene, held at Good Shepherd Church in Beverly Hills. Cooper was best man. "In spite of great pain, Poppa wanted to be there for Fred," his friend since *High Noon*, writes Maria. Later, at the Coopers' home the couples "toasted life and celebrated love."[26]

On Monday, April 17, a visibly moved Jimmy Stewart appeared at the Academy Awards to accept his friend's honorary Oscar. "We're all proud of you, Coop. We're all so very proud," he said, after which, Maria writes, "Jimmy started to break down, and that was the first the public knew that 'Coop' was getting ready for his last ride home."[27]

"I'll get this to you right away," Stewart said in closing. "And, Coop I want you to know, that with this goes all the warm friendship and the affection and the admiration and the deep respect of all of us."

The next day, newspaper headlines around the world blared, "Gary Cooper has cancer."

Visitors started coming to the Cooper's home in Holmby Hills, and messages poured in from friends and well-wishers around the world, including Pope John XXIII, Queen Elizabeth, John Wayne, Hemingway, former President Dwight Eisenhower, Bob Hope, Audrey Hepburn, and many others. Even President John F. Kennedy called from Washington, finally getting through after a day of trying.

Gary and Rocky Cooper in the last few weeks of his life, with his scapular medal clearly visible

Friends, expecting to find gloom at the Cooper home, instead found light and sunshine, crisp flowers and cheerful music, as the family faced this profoundly difficult time with faith. Billy Wilder, Meyers writes, "recalled that [Cooper] dressed in stylish pajamas and robe and seemed more composed than his guests." Rocky later spoke with Hedda Hopper, who reported that she said of her husband, "He'd been perfectly wonderful throughout the entire illness" and that "what helped him most was his religion." As the cancer progressed, "He never asked 'Why me?' and never complained." Furthermore, she said, he was spiritually enriched by the sacraments and books such as Bishop Fulton Sheen's *Peace of Soul* and Thomas Merton's *No Man Is an Island*.

The first week of May, Hemingway memoirist A.E. Hotchner visited Cooper, who appeared "a wasted figure, lying immobile in his darkened room." Coop told him "Papa" had called him a couple weeks before to inform him he was sick, as well. As he said this, he kept pausing, Hotchner writes, because it was so painful to speak. Mustering his dwindling energy, Coop said he told him,

"I bet I beat you to the barn."[28] Then, he asked if Hemingway was back at the Mayo clinic, which Hotchner confirmed. With that, the drama heightened:

> He was hit by a big pain and his face contorted as he fought it off; sweat instantly covered his face. When the pain had passed, Cooper reached his hand over to the bed table and picked up a crucifix, which he put on the pillow beside his head.
>
> "Please give Papa a message. It's important and you mustn't forget because I'll not be talking to him again. Tell him...that time I wondered if I made the right decision" (regarding his conversion)—he moved the crucifix a little closer so that it touched his cheek—"tell him it was the best thing I ever did."
>
> "I'll tell him."
>
> "Don't forget."
>
> "Don't worry, Coops, I'll tell him."[29]

Both Cooper and Hemingway shared the habit of carrying small wooden crucifixes in their pockets.

"I know," announced Cooper as he lay dying, "that what is happening is God's will. I am not afraid of the future."[30]

Gary Cooper died of prostate and colon cancer on May 13, 1961, Feast of Our Lady of Fatima, six weeks before Hemingway died.[31] He is beloved for the indelible portrait he gave us of what it is to be an authentic American hero—a portrait that's incomplete without the story of his last days.

Chapter Four

• • •

BOB HOPE AND
HIS LADIES OF HOPE

• • •

The smartest thing Bob Hope ever
did was marry Dolores.[1]

—LUCILLE BALL

One of the great things about my
mother is she never stopped encour-
aging us.[2]

—BOB HOPE

Bob Hope excelled at everything he did. And he did it all—theater,
radio, film, TV, philanthropy, business, service to country—in
unparalleled fashion. According to *The Guinness Book of World
Records*, he was history's "most honored entertainer."[3]

He was, of course, devoted to the troops, doing 199 USO shows
around the globe over half a century, from World War II through
Desert Storm, sometimes at great risk. For his efforts, President
John F. Kennedy awarded him the Congressional Gold Medal in
1963, President Lyndon Baines Johnson presented him with the
Medal of Freedom in 1969, and the U.S. Congress declared him
"First and Only Honorary Veteran of the U.S. Armed Forces" in
1997.

One show, in particular, demonstrated his mettle. It was
Christmas Eve 1983, not long after terrorists had bombed the Beirut
barracks housing the Multinational Force in Lebanon—killing

220 U.S. marines, 18 sailors, and 3 soldiers. Bob Hope thought they should go to Beirut to boost morale, his publicist Harry Flynn said. And while they usually performed aboard ships, anchored off the Mediterranean's Eastern Coast, this time, a determined Hope somehow got permission to bring the show ashore—a closely held secret until they arrived.

While they were flying in, aboard a CH46 with four SEALS sitting on the floor toting automatic weapons, going in "real low because of heat-seeking missiles that could take helicopters out," said Flynn, one of the SEALS wanted to know if Hope was scared.

"Of *what*?" asked Hope. "That's the way he was," said Flynn. He fearlessly stared down terrorists—and anyone or anything that got in his way.[4]

Confronting his own demons? That was another matter.

He had excelled at everything—not always a source of undiluted pleasure for his wife Dolores. But in the waning days of his life, he finally set things right.

Growing Up with Hope

The fifth of seven boys, Bob Hope was born Leslie Townes Hope on May 29, 1903, in Eltham, England, some ten miles from London's Charing Cross Station.

His Welsh mother, Avis Townes Hope—born in 1873, orphaned when her parents drowned at sea—was devoted and loving. His English father, William Henry "Harry" Hope, a stonecutter, born in 1870, "had only one fault," Hope writes in his 1954 memoir: "It was his theory that, as a result of his occupation, stone dust collected in his throat. He stopped off at the pubs to sluice it off."[5]

It was not always that way. When his parents wed on April 25, 1891, in Cardiff, Wales, Harry was hardworking and temperate and made a nice home with ponies and lush gardens. But his trade gradually proved financially inadequate—bricks displacing stone masonry by 1900—and, when out of work, Harry would bet on the horses and ply himself with alcohol, worsening the family's financial straits. This heightened tensions at home, leading to the harsh discipline of his sons.

Their only daughter, Emily, born in 1895, died of diphtheria in 1898, while Avis was pregnant with William John ("Jack"), having given birth to Frederick Charles in the intervening years. Ivor and Jim were the eldest. This tragedy escalated the family's downward spiral—Avis plunging into depression, Harry drinking and gambling more heavily. Financially strapped, they moved to Eltham into inexpensive homes Harry's father had built. But work soon dried up and, besides drinking and gambling, Harry began romancing young women—to feel like a man, bury his feelings of inadequacy, and anesthetize the pain over Emily's loss. His wife, discovering a barmaid's photo in his wallet, hit him so hard he nearly died.

She finally forgave him, if never quite forgetting, and in 1903, while England was suffering a debilitating depression, she gave birth to her sixth child—Leslie. A year later, the family moved to the resort town of Harry's childhood, though jobs were scarce. To help financially, Avis cashiered at a tea shop, bringing Leslie along. She cleaned houses too, taking time out to give birth to Sidney in 1905. At night, to lift the family's spirits, she would play the spinet and sing Welsh songs.

In the spring of 1906, Harry, now in Bristol, but faring no better, heard about America's abundance from his brother. After fraught discussion and tearful departing hugs, he emigrated to Cleveland, plunging Avis into another depression. But Harry's promising letters brightened her spirits, and, two years later, she and the six children made the arduous fourteen-day journey to America, each wearing layers of clothes. They arrived at Ellis Island on March 30, 1908.

Once in Cleveland, it soon became apparent that not only was the weather colder in America, so too, were the manners: Nice guys finished last in this fast-rising industrial colossus—now enduring a severe economic contraction in the wake of the 1907 Bankers' Panic. Easing the financial stress, Avis rented a more spacious home so she could rent to boarders, guaranteeing a monthly income, and to make room for their last child, George Percy, born in 1909. The grown boys chipped in too, taking part-time jobs to enrich the family coffers. While working as a paper boy, Hope met John D. Rockefeller, who counseled him: "Trust nobody. Never give credit and always keep change on hand."[6] Sage advice he never forgot.

Of his early religious formation, he writes: "Mom...after making sure we were clean and uncomfortably dressed...sent us off to Sunday school at the Euclid Avenue Presbyterian—a church dad had helped build."[7] (She found the local Episcopalian church too upper crusty.) And, while she "frowned on card playing, cigarettes, and public dancing," writes biographer Richard Zoglin,[8] spiritual exercises beyond Sunday services seemed a remote concern, given the immediacy of just surviving. As a child, Hope was rescued by his brother Ivor when he got pinned under a pier and nearly drowned. And while he survived his father's brutal beatings physically, it was his mother who worked to save him psychologically.

A singer herself, Avis encouraged her favorite son's theatrical talent early on—starting with spinet lessons in England—and scrimped to buy him a secondhand upright piano so he could resume lessons in America. Leslie, determined to avoid his father's fate, developed his talents, winning a Charlie Chaplin contest in 1915, using the prize money to buy his mother a new stove. From then on, he set his cap—later his trademark brown derby hat—for the theater, far from the drab, workaday world, convinced that being on stage was his true calling.

He rose up by dint of hard work, starting in vaudeville in 1924 with partner Lloyd "Lefty" Durbin. In 1925, scandal-tainted Fatty Arbuckle got them steady work in "Hurley's Jolly Follies" on the small-time, Ohio-based Gus Sun Circuit. "I was making forty dollars a week and sending twenty home to my mother to help out."[9] When Lloyd died midseason of tuberculosis, Hurley found Hope's new partner—a likeable guy and swell dancer named George Byrne, whom Hope described as "pink cheeked and naïve...real quiet. Real Ohio."[10]

The pace was intense, conditions often squalid, but he always kept a chipper spirit in spite of setbacks along the way. After landing small, short-lived roles on Broadway in *Sidewalks of New York* (1927–1928) and *Ups-a-Daisy* (1928), their star dimmed, prompting a William Morris agent to tell them, "You ought to go West, change your act get a new start."[11]

It was in New Castle, Pennsylvania, that Hope got his solo break when, at the end of a three-day engagement, he was tapped to introduce the next week's show. He told a well-received Scotch joke, and kept adding more each time. The audience howled, prompting the manager to tell him he should be an emcee.

In 1928, after trying out his act in Cleveland, he headed for mob-ruled Chicago at the height of the Roaring Twenties, to go solo. But after running up a four-hundred-dollar tab for donuts and coffee (and Prohibition-era medicinal spirits, too, no doubt)—and changing his name to the more masculine "Lester"—he wasn't making it.

On the verge of giving up, he bumped into a Cleveland friend named Charlie, who introduced him to "another Charlie" (Hogan, a theater booker), who asked him, "'How'd you like to play the West Englewood Theater Decoration Day? [Memorial Day] Would twenty-five dollars be all right?'" "I just managed to say, 'I'll take it,' without bursting into tears," he writes.[12] Soon Hogan booked him at the Stratford to serve as emcee for the vaudeville show, complementing the silent film *Dressed to Kill* (1928), starring Mary Astor. His two-week engagement was extended to six months. He was on his way.

In 1929, the well-known and well-liked performer arrived in New York—now as "Bob Hope," suggesting a "Hi ya, fellas" regular guy.[13] He soon signed with the B.F. Keith Agency for three years, edging them up to $450 a week after he turned in a masterful performance at the cavernous Proctor's Eighty-Sixth, the toughest crowd in New York. His first national tour on the Keith-Orpheum vaudeville circuit, 1929–1930, featured his "Keep Smiling" act.[14] They booked him twice at New York's Palace Theatre, vaudeville's pinnacle, in 1931 and 1932. A Broadway return wasn't far behind—starting with some small roles.

Pivotal Roberta

Soon, he was offered the role of Huckleberry Haines in Jerome Kerns's smash hit *Roberta*, playing from November 1933 to July 1934. It catalyzed a host of other opportunities in radio, film, and TV, starting with NBC's Bromo-Seltzer Show on radio in late 1935, kicking off a sixty-year affiliation.[15] Hollywood wasn't far behind. In 1937, Paramount cast him in *The Big Broadcast of*

1938. By 1950, he was doing TV. His first special, "Star Spangled Review," debuted on Easter Sunday. Then there were more theatrical appearances, including at the London Palladium in 1951.[16]

Early on, his *Roberta* costar, George Murphy, took him to the Vogue Club on Fifty-Seventh Street to introduce him to a beautiful singer named Dolores Reade, whose Italian-American father was a well-known "singing waiter" on 149th Street in the Bronx, said Fr. Benedict Groeschel.[17] Her mother was an Irish-American beauty; *she* was irresistible.

Bob fell in love with Dolores when she sang in her "low, husky voice...soft and sweet.... 'It's Only a Paper Moon' and 'Did You Ever See a Dream Walking?'[18] They wed a few months later on February 19, 1934, in Cleveland, though there was no marriage certificate. However, one existed for an earlier marriage, also in Cleveland, to former vaudeville partner Grace Louise Troxnell, on January 25, 1933, which Arthur Marx, son of Groucho, discovered in the course of writing his unauthorized Hope biography.[19] The details of that marriage—why it occurred and whether, or how long, they actually lived as husband and wife—are murky except to say it was an unhappy union. A divorce was granted on November 19, 1934. The engagement of Bob and Dolores was first announced in New York on August 4, 1934.[20] Their union, rare in Hollywood annals, lasted sixty-nine years, during which they welcomed four adopted children—Linda, Anthony, Eleanora Avis (Nora), and Kelly.

Starting in World War II, Hope began donating entertainment hours to cheer up the troops—starting with his first performance in May 1941 at California's March Field. He was hooked. But, in typical Hope fashion, he didn't stop there. Cerebral palsy was soon on his radar, followed by the Eisenhower Medical Center in

Palm Springs, for which he donated the land and raised millions through his Annual Hope Golf Classic, with Dolores chairing the board. And there were numerous other causes—most notably Catholic charitable works, especially those benefiting children and the poor.

Besides his indefatigable energy, he now had great wealth to bring to these causes. As Marx writes of Hope, by the midpoint of his life, he was "no longer just a comedian or film star. He was big business—oil, real estate, frozen orange juice, charity fund-raising, golf, wholesale meat, personal appearances on both sides of the Atlantic." His investments even included major league baseball. Hope bought a five-percent interest in his favorite ball team, the Cleveland Indians, in 1949. He was also part owner of several radio and TV stations."[21]

His success was accompanied, and made possible, by a fiercely competitive spirit, combined with a penny-pinching nature—a remnant of his struggle just to survive as a child and in vaudeville.

While he had a heart of gold when it came to the troops, special charities, and special friends (e.g., paying his agent Jack Saphier's entire medical bill when he was terminally ill), he drove hard bargains with others, particularly his writers. For instance, he wrote into writers' contracts they could pick up their option only two weeks into the season. If the writer didn't renew a contract, it would be too late to find other work.

Similarly, after long sessions with writers on the *Bob Hope Pepsodent Show*, he would routinely ask junior writer Sherwood Schwartz (known for *Gilligan's Island*), to get him a pineapple sundae, which Hope would then enjoy, as his hungry writers salivated.[22] But they loved him just the same. They must have sensed that, as Zoglin writes, "that protective shell" had something to do with his hardscrabble early childhood, so devoid of stable attachments, and not wanting to suffer their loss again.[23] The love was on display when Schwartz was posted with Armed Forces Radio in New York City during World War II. Learning that Hope was doing a *Pepsodent Show* there, he bought a pineapple sundae at Schrafft's on Madison Avenue and snuck up behind Hope during the rehearsal break at the NBC Studio. "'Here's our sundae, Mr. Hope' [he said] and put it in his hand. Without turning around, and without missing a beat, Hope took the sundae" from Schwartz, and snapped, "What kept you so long, kid?"[24]

All through his life, he was also a prodigious womanizer— often leaving Dolores in tears. "I'm no angel. I've known very few angels," Hope writes.[25] As Marx summed it up, the scuttlebutt is he had more women than Errol Flynn, Chico Marx, and his close friend Bing Crosby combined, which once brought the couple to the brink of divorce.[26]

"Dolores," writes Marx, "told friends she continually sought God's assistance in helping her deal with Hope's philandering, and went to St. Charles Church on Lankersham Boulevard and Moorpark, in North Hollywood, every day. There she'd fall to her knees, and pray" for Bob's conversion…but "he wasn't about to be converted to Catholicism, though he told *TV Guide* he was religious in his own way."[27]

The irony is, Bob Hope's signature song, "Thanks for the Memory," is about a couple that is contemplating divorce. Then, they begin to reminisce about the wonderful times they've had and decide to stay together. Dolores toughed it out, knowing infidelity was Bob's weakness—albeit, like his good qualities, it played out in extreme ways.

And the Hopes had some wonderful times. "When we were celebrating our 50th anniversary," Dolores said, "people would say, 'Fifty years?' And Bob would say, 'Yeah, but I've only been home three weeks.'" To mark that half-century, she gave him a paperweight inscribed, "Don't think these three weeks haven't been fun."[28]

It wasn't entirely in jest. "I'm pretty sure I'm seventy-five,' Hope said at his birthday tribute after all the toasts, having imbibed perhaps one too many. "But, I've lied to so many girls. Of course, they always find out about one a.m. Dolores that's a joke."[29]

Dolores toughed it out knowing infidelity was Bob's weakness—albeit, like his good qualities, it played out in extreme ways. Also, she knew she was the most beautiful compared to the other women he strayed with—and that she was his wife, after all.

Agent of Conversion

"Dolores," Fr. Groeschel said, "faithfully, prayerfully, patiently, and with a certain amount of suffering" endured these trials. "She was a devout Christian wife, and she did what she was supposed to do." Quite simply, the reason she was able to persevere, he said, is that "Dolores Hope was a great Christian."

Through it all, she was praying him into the Church.

"Basically, the agent of his conversion was his wife," said Cardinal Theodore McCarrick, the retired archbishop of Washington, who got to know Hope through Cardinal Terence Cooke of New York when he served as his secretary. She was a daily communicant and was devoted to Our Lady. And she prayed for Bob with a deep faith, asking others to pray for him as well.[30] Also—and this is not to be underestimated—"she took very good care of him," longtime friend Virginia Zamboni said.

Father Groeschel observed this transformation up close.

"They were both very friendly people," said Groeschel and

would occasionally open their "large" yet "comfortable" home to guests.

"Bob," he said, "was very pleasant and easy to get on with." He loved to tell a story to priests who visited, sometimes for retreats Dolores hosted, about a "big Catholic" event he attended, where "the priest who was introducing him told eight jokes. So Bob got up, looked at the crowd," as if warming up to tell his own set of jokes, "and said, 'Let us pray.' That," said Groeschel, "is real Bob Hope!"

In the midst of the mirth, Groeschel said, Hope was "extremely respectful to [me as] a priest. Practically every word or sentence, he would call me 'Father.'"

Of course, it's quite comical to imagine Bob Hope—so firmly planted in the here and now, not missing a beat when it came to human nature—reacting to all of the reminders of eternity around him.

Sometimes, the two intersected, exemplified by this note from Dolores to Fr. George Rutler in 1991: "One of the times I was watching you on EWTN," she writes, "you told a wonderful story about St. Philip Neri, who died with a Bible and a joke book along side of him.... I told Bob about this, and he asked if there really was such a joke book. Is it possible that anything like this can be traced?"[31]

They shared more than laughs with their friends.

"They were very generous in every way," said McCarrick. "The many benefactions are legion." For example, the Hopes endowed Our Lady of Hope Chapel in memory of Bob's mother, Avis. It was dedicated in May 1994 at the National Shrine of the Immaculate Conception, some sixty years after her death. And,

Groeschel said, "They supported many works of the Franciscan Friars of the Renewal."

God was generous, too.

Arc of Conversion

The arc of Bob Hope's conversion is apparent in *My Life in Jokes*, his last book, divided into ten decades. Introducing his forties, he writes: "I was offering time and laughs—the men and women fighting the war were offering up their lives. They taught me what sacrifice was all about."[32]

It was during World War II, said McCarrick, that Bob became "very close" to New York Cardinal Francis Spellman. "They made all those rounds visiting the troops. And I really think that Bob was impressed by the faith of the Catholic men and women in the service that he met and by their enthusiasm to greet Cardinal Spellman. He often said, 'He got a bigger hand than I did.'"

"For many years," McCarrick said, "we had been chatting with him about the Church."

Though he liked to quip he was a "comedian by religion," gradually, he began to see the dimension of faith in his life—perhaps aided, ironically enough, by ailments of the eye.[33] His left eye and then his right would hemorrhage·and he would often have to rest in a dark room after surgery—once for three weeks. For the peripatetic Hope, that must have been pure agony. But it provided a badly needed time for reflection.

In his late eighties, he got the ultimate wake-up call. It was at the festivities surrounding the opening of the Ronald Reagan Presidential Foundation and Library on November 4, 1991. For the first time in his life, he was not given VIP treatment. "He couldn't believe it," Marx writes. "'I'm Bob Hope,' he complained to the people in charge… 'I'm sure I'm on the limo list.'"[34]

But he wasn't.

This world-class comedian and philanthropist, who had jour-
neyed the world many times over, flying "a few million miles,"
since World War II, entertaining "his boys," this friend of presidents and royalty since the forties—who had "known most of
the great personalities of our
time, in politics, sports and
show business," this outsized
personality of whom President
Johnson had said, "With his
gifts of joy to all the American
people, he has written his
name large in the history of
our times," was now being
shunted aside to make small

Bob and Dolores Hope

talk on an open-air tram with Lou Wasserman and Michael Eisner
on the way to celebrating Reagan's immortalization at his brand-
new library![35]

After all these years of self-indulgence—interlaced with great
generosity—it was as if God was tapping Bob on the shoulder to
give him a pineapple ice-cream sundae of a spiritual sort.

In his last ten years, Bob Hope finally settled down and began
enjoying life with Dolores.

Once Larry King asked him, as recounted by Marx, "'Bob, and
I want you to be truthful. You've worked with beautiful women
all your life. Didn't you ever find it tempting?'

Hope squirmed uncomfortably in his chair...[and, without the
aid of writers] finally replied, 'Yes, but I always wind up coming
back to Dolores.'"[36]

The old duffer also began attending church regularly with her at St. Charles Borromeo in North Hollywood, a few blocks from their home on Moorpark Street, at the corner of Lankershim Avenue.

"Dolores," McCarrick said, "always was anxious that he become a Catholic. I think he had been close to the Church in faith for many years…and she was the one who kept bringing it up to him as a possibility. She would never force anyone. She was always very thoughtful and considerate. But she was persistent in saying, 'One of these days; one of these days.' And, finally, he said, 'Okay, it's time.'"

Fr. Groeschel said that while Bob Hope was advanced in age (ninety-three) when he converted, "he was very clear," and, "could talk."

Msgr. Thomas Kiefer, former pastor of St. Charles Borromeo (1984–2000), and "a dear friend of both of them," said McCarrick, "was the one who ultimately brought him into the Church."

Bob Hope died on July 27, 2003, at age one hundred. Eight years later, on September 19, 2011, at age 102, Dolores Hope breathed her last.

Late in the summer of 2011, Father Groeschel stopped by to see her.

"Dolores, I hope you're living comfortably," he said.

"I'm ready to get out of here comfortably," she answered.

Knowing she had helped her husband win the biggest prize of all must have been great comfort, indeed.

Chapter Five

* * *

MARY ASTOR: BECOMING A
STAR...AND A SAINT

* * *

The most glorious experience of my
life was finding Faith.[1]

—MARY ASTOR

Mary Astor, an all-American, self-assured beauty, with a hint of pathos, left an indelible imprint on the American psyche. Who can forget her performances in *The Maltese Falcon* (1941), *Meet Me in St. Louis* (1944), or *The Great Lie* (1941)?

She found God, by accident, just before she hit her professional stride, reveling in her newfound faith, as if on a "pink cloud," she writes, only to 'backslide,' when life got tough.[2] By age fifty, she was drinking uncontrollably to relieve a pain she could not name. *What was it?* she prayed.

A Lonely Child

Born Lucile Vasconcellos Langhanke on May 3, 1906, in Quincy, Illinois, she was the only child of Otto Ludwig Wilhelm Langhanke and Helen Vasconcellos.

Her first five years were spent in a small, dingy flat above a saloon.

Otto had immigrated from Berlin in 1889 at age eighteen, crossing the Atlantic in steerage, dreaming of America's gold-paved streets. Once in New York City, his halting English and paltry savings sent him packing for Lawrence, Kansas, a German immigrant enclave, where he enrolled in the University of Kansas. He met his wife, ten years his junior, in a Topeka clothing store, where he worked summers. The oldest of six children, she was raised on a farm in Lyons, Kansas, where the couple wed on August 3, 1904.

Her mother's world was as "narrow and limited" as her father's was "broad and varied," Mary writes in *My Story: An Autobiography*.[3] But Otto was stubborn, chasing one elusive scheme after another. A word, noise, or gesture would enrage him, sending him storming out of the room, leaving his wife in tears. Helen, for her part, resented Lucile from the start, as her diary revealed. In this environment, Lucile took to spending time alone—under a bed or in a darkened closet, where she was often sent as punishment, frequently finding restful sleep instead.

In the summer of 1913, the family moved to a farm with a large mid-Victorian mansion, where, she writes, her "real memories" began. She loved to roam the lush countryside in her sandals and overalls, collie in tow—escaping to Cedar Creek, with its great "hideaways" that afforded her the pleasures of skipping stones, watching minnows, and luxuriating in the gurgling water and gleaming sun, while living in the fairy tale world of the stories she read.[4] Meanwhile, Otto became increasingly angry as a walnut grove investment and other schemes dried up and, with the impending war, he lost his teaching job—poultry farming becoming their sole source of sustenance.[5] As the leaves turned, activity shifted inside—heightening tensions, until happily relieved at the two-room country schoolhouse called Highland School.

In 1916, a piano arrived on her tenth birthday—her father insisting she become a great pianist. From that point forward, she writes, the relationship devolved into one of "fearful respect."[6] Making matters worse, that fall, the family moved back downtown after Otto was reinstated into his teaching job. One day, she stopped practicing piano as she dreamed about the country, prompting her father to gently ask, "Don't you want to *be* somebody?" To which she replied, "I *am* somebody, I am myself." She joyfully added her goals—education, work then marriage and having children, which, to her shock, elicited a thunderous lecture punctuated with phrases like "good-for-nothing," while her mother pleaded for him not to hurt her.[7]

A Blossoming Beauty

Lucile's years on the farm had given her a natural beauty that set her apart from the affectatious "town girls,"[8] which attracted the boys and gave birth to "the Great Idea."[9] Forget piano—Lucile would become an actress. She loved the silent pictures and the stars, an enthusiasm she shared with her next-door neighbor, Marian, her first real friend—her parents approving of the friendship "even though she was Catholic."[10]

"In the strange and inscrutable working of Providence," Mary writes, "our childish game of mailing coupons…led me to a career as an actress." They began entering contests, initially for bicycles and, one day, Lucile noticed *Motion Picture Magazine*'s contest to find "the beauty in our land" and decided to give it a shot. Almost immediately, the magazine published her photo, along with the month's other seven, captioned: "This month's fame and fortune winners." Of four finalists annually, one was promised a studio contract.

While Lucile was merely "pleased and flattered,"[11] her father sold all the furniture to finance a frenzied move to Chicago in the spring of 1917, wearing mother and daughter "to a dull, uncomprehending fatigue."[12] But there was no arguing. For Otto, to plan was to act. His first-year German text and teacher's manual, published just as America entered World War I, was a flop. But Lucile had star quality.

Initially, their time in Chicago at East Forty-Seventh Street was "a dreary and unhappy time," she writes, amid South Side neighborhood toughies and hardboiled Chicago-native teachers at the nearby public school, where she was finishing sixth grade.[13] Otto barely eked out a living, so Helen got a job teaching English literature and drama at Kenwood-Loring School for Girls, which Lucile attended tuition-free. "I loved the school," she writes. "I felt I was learning again." Meanwhile, Otto focused on making Lucile a star, happily answering "sucker ads."[14]

Lucile, with her big brown doe eyes, engaging smile, polish, and sophistication, began attracting more male admirers, prompting her worried father one night to explain the 'facts of life' so crassly that it created in Lucile a "revulsion and disgust and terror," affecting her physically and emotionally.[15] Over the next four years, shy and withdrawn, she pursued many one-sided relationships with men, mostly World War I veterans, some wounded— always older. In June 1919, after she graduated from elementary school, her father isolated her further by taking over her education with accredited coursework from the Horace Mann correspondence school.

Acting became Mary's outlet. She studied at a drama school, run by Helen's friend Bertha Iles, an attractive, happy woman with infectious laughter, who knew her craft and had the students perform at various World War–related benefits and fundraisers, where Lucile commanded returning soldiers' attention. But commanding the attention of movie directors was another matter.

So, in early 1920, she competed once more in the *Motion Picture Magazine* contest—and, this time, was chosen as a finalist, then a runner-up.

Her father seized the opportunity and, in June 1920, as before, abruptly moved the family—this time to New York, where they walked tirelessly, seeking out auditions and a place to stay—finally finding a small apartment on 110th Street. Her father immediately began hounding *Motion Picture Magazine* editor Eugene Brewster, who finally granted Lucile an interview and screen test at his Roslyn estate. And off they went.

Lights, Camera, Action

The grounds had been transformed into a small movie set. Away from this sideshow, Lucile met renowned fashion photographer Charles Albin, who felt "Rusty" (Lucile's nickname) had a "Madonna quality."[16] She loved the fact he had worked with her idol, Lillian Gish, and by day's end, had landed a screen test with D.W. Griffith.

At Griffith's studio, a twenty-eight-acre estate in Mamaroneck, Gish immediately set the budding actress's mind at ease. But after a wearying day of filming, the call never came, Lucile later learned, because Griffith deemed Otto too anxious. Meanwhile, Albin asked her to pose for him, as Otto began peddling his literary wares. One day while he was visiting Famous Players-Lasky Studios in Astoria, Harry Durant noticed Lucile's portfolio tucked under his arm and summoned her to their offices, where she was greeted by Jesse Lasky, Walter Wanger, and Louella Parsons. They immediately changed her name to Mary Astor, gave her a new wardrobe and hairstyle to match, and, by day's end, offered her a six-month contract for sixty dollars a week. Her father became her business manager.

Life was changing fast. Mary Astor was instructed to show up for work at the year-old Astoria studio and at the age of fourteen, she made her debut in *The Scarecrow* (1920). But they let her contract lapse, providentially so, for she landed a starring role in a series of movie shorts based on famous paintings, including the two-reeler *The Beggar Maid* (1921), which led to her first feature-length movie, *John Smith* (1922).

Escape to Hollywood

In 1923, Otto, sensing Mary's star was rising, moved the family out to Hollywood. Initially, studio-hopping, while playing ever larger roles, Famous Players-Lasky re-signed her, this time to a one-year five-hundred-dollar-a-week contract. With studios on both coasts, Mary crisscrossed the country with her canary, Tweetums, while her father pocketed her earnings. A virtual prisoner in her own home, she would desperately escape, just as she had as a child—only this time it was into the mysterious adult world, where she "rushed headlong into nothing but trouble."[17]

The first trouble came in the form of legendary actor John Barrymore, twenty-four years her senior. Separated from his wife, he spotted beautiful seventeen-year-old Mary in a movie magazine and sought her out for his next film, Warner Bros.'s *Beau Brummel* (1924). Famous Players consented and the two actors began an affair—made possible because Mary's parents let Barrymore give her "acting lessons" in private. Her parents knew what was going on, yet did nothing to stop it. "He seldom drank around me," she writes. "His language…was often strong, but it was never filthy… he gave me a love, wholehearted and undemanding, such as I had never known before."[18]

In 1925, while the affair was ongoing, Mary's parents purchased "Moorcrest," a grandiose Moorish mansion, which Charlie

Chaplin had previously lived in, set atop the Hollywood Hills in a utopian "Theosophist" colony. Marie and Harry Hotchener, both prominent Theosophists, became friends, and Marie intervened when tensions rose, negotiating Mary's right to work unchaperoned and to earn a meager weekly allowance. Then, after Mary fled to a Hollywood hotel after escaping through the mansion's second-floor window, Marie persuaded Otto to give his nineteen-year-old daughter a five-hundred-dollar savings account and freedom to come and go as she pleased.

When the affair with Barrymore ended in 1926, she was heartbroken. The hurt was compounded when Warner Bros. cast her opposite her former lover, this time in *Don Juan* (1926), which also costarred his new flame, Dolores Costello, Mary's fellow WAMPAS[19] Baby Star, who now occupied the privileged seat on set next to Barrymore. After *Don Juan* premiered on August 6, 1926, making movie history for its Vitaphone recording of background music and sound, Mary joined *Rough Riders* (1926), the location set barreling into hot, dusty San Antonio on August 19, 1926. Accorded honorary membership in the First Brigade Calvary Regiment, it was a whole new world, helping ease the pain of her eighteen-month adulterous affair. "We were lionized, partied, dated" nonstop, she writes, of this Barrymore-free setting, where she began smoking, wearing lip rouge, taking an occasional drink, and dating Rhodes Scholar and Olympic diving champion John Monk Saunders, author of *Wings*, simultaneously being filmed in San Antonio.[20]

True Love

No sooner had filming wrapped in late November 1926, than she met Ken Hawks, brother of up-and-coming director Howard Hawks. They made a cute couple at golf tournaments and film premieres and were soon engaged. Mary, not wanting to keep anything from him, confessed to him about her "long, desperate affair" with Barrymore, but Ken, though shocked, decided he loved her.[21] Nothing else mattered.

She was growing up fast and began making professional decisions herself—one day simply informing her father she was switching to make a picture for United Artists.

As the months passed, she also began keeping a diary, writing of her love for Ken, though admitting the long engagement, which would last thirteen months, was difficult for her, given their resolve to stay chaste until marriage.[22] But, if their romantic life had limits, their social life continued unabated—including the wedding of Norma Shearer and Irving Thaalberg and the season opening of the Mayfair Club, where, she writes, for the first time in her life she had too much to drink and had her first hangover, which Ken helped her weather.

Shortly after Ken's long-term Fox contract materialized, they finally wed at Moorcrest on February 24, 1928. Later that night, Ken simply kissed his bride goodnight and that was that. "A bit tearfully," she writes, "I fell asleep."[23]

Shortly afterward the couple settled into their home on Alcyona Drive and Mary starred in *Dressed to Kill* (1928) on loan to Fox. She received such good reviews that when her Warner contract ended, Fox picked her up for $3,750 a week. Later that year, she starred in the studio's sophisticated comedy *Dry Martini* (1928), which recreated the libertine atmosphere of 1920s Paris, including illicit affairs, which she found a refreshing new perspective. "With its specious doctrine of self-indulgence," she writes, "it rushed into the vacuum of my moral sense and captivated me completely."[24]

With the consummation of her marriage yet to occur, and

without any moral underpinnings, Mary fell headlong into infidelity with another Fox executive, Russell Bradbury, and became pregnant. She decided to have an abortion as "good taste," she writes, called for. The "properly exclusive establishment" she went to "committed such crimes under the fiction of 'therapeutic treatment'" giving her, she writes, "a new burden of guilt to carry."[25] Soon, she began having tiffs with Ken, now drinking heavily and suffering bouts of dysentery, which, she later learned from her mother's diary, were due to a childhood illness and the fact that he was also tortured by her infidelity, which Helen had told him about. Nonetheless, he had forgiven her.

Before long, they became engulfed in the difficult transition to "talkies"—Mary failing the Fox sound test. Released from her contract, she was adrift for eight months, while the couple moved into a new home near the top of Lookout Mountain above Beverly Hills. Her welcome gift: a realtor trying to blackmail Mary over her affair with Bradbury. Calling his bluff, she picked up the phone to call Ken, rendering the photos worthless.

Life was good. Ken was making mounds of money in the stock market and was now a Fox director, fulfilling his longtime ambition. Mary took up painting and began socializing with writer Marian Spitzer and her interesting, intelligent friends at her patented dinner parties—one night featuring a newcomer named Bob Hope and his song "Thanks for the Memory." "The stimulation of the mind," she writes, "seemed to lessen the nagging of the body."[26] Then, Florence Eldridge, wife of Frederick March, invited her to meet Edward Everett Horton, from which flowed a starring role in the play *Among the Married*. While it only paid $150 a week, it broke Mary's streak of bad luck and paved her way back into films.

Twists and Turns

As the 1930s dawned, Ken was scheduled to film a parachute drop and assured Mary it would be safe. That morning, the day after New Year's, holding her kitten, she waved good-bye to him. It would be her last time. Later that day, Ken's plane, a Stinson SM-IF Detroiter, collided with an identical plane, while filming over the Pacific Ocean in the glaring sun. He died on impact, along with eight others.

As if the shock of losing him were not enough, she was also in desperate financial straits. Ken had just lost the lion's share of his investments in the recent stock market crash and had no life insurance. But Mary would not return to her parents' home, nor would she remain in their home on Lookout Mountain. Instead, she rented a place at La Leyenda Apartments in Hollywood and prepared for her first picture at Paramount (formerly Famous Players)—and life without Ken. Also, in June 1930, she relieved her father of his business management role. In ten years, she had grossed close to half a million dollars, of which she had saved just three thousand.

Then, one day she noticed an unusual rash. The physician who examined her told her she was run-down, having returned to work too soon after Ken's death. He prescribed rest, "a glass of milk every half hour, mineral oil, complete bed rest, and sun on the roof."[27] She was to have no visitors except for her maid, no phone calls, no cigarettes, and no liquor. After about five days, she was finally able to relax, unwind, and rest.

Mary, now twenty-four, had been distancing herself from her old friends. They reminded her too much of Ken. Into the void stepped her doctor, Franklyn Thorpe. Twelve years her senior, he was gentle, soft-spoken and intense, and loved surgery, though not the business side. While a less-than-perfect match, they wed on June 29, 1931, Mary vowing to make it work. At the same time, she landed a contract with RKO Radio Pictures Inc., and made film after film—*Behind Office Doors*, *The Sin Ship*, *Smart Woman*, and *Men of Chance*—in 1931 alone. She also became pregnant in the fall. Later, while enduring the last difficult weeks of pregnancy, she sailed with Franklyn to Hawaii. Predictably, she became ill and, on June 15, 1932, while recuperating in that exotic paradise, gave birth to her daughter, Marylyn Hauoli Thorpe. But Mary soon tired of Franklyn's overly serious nature and fled to New York, where she was introduced to and began an affair with the playwright George S. Kaufman.

Life with Franklyn had become "a series of explosions," she writes, and they divorced in 1935, teeing up a ferocious custody battle.[28] Her diary, which she realized belatedly could serve as fodder in a trial, had news about prominent Hollywood figures. Though it had been altered and the most salacious parts were pure fiction, careers were nonetheless ruined. In the summer of 1936, while the trial was held at night, Mary filmed *Dodsworth* (1936) during the day, playing Mrs. Edith Cortright. The singular news focus during that time was "Mary Astor's diary."[29] In the end, she got what she sought—custody of her daughter, Marylyn—while the judge, deeming the diary unfit to read, ordered it incinerated.

With that chapter closed, a new one was about to open at a party hosted by *Dodsworth* costar Ruth Chatterton, where Mary met the famous English director, Auriol Lee, who talked up his British friend "Manuelito," who had attended Cambridge for a time, until family funds ran out, subsequently serving as a bank clerk in Mexico City. He was now Auriol's secretary. The night they met, Mary, now thirty, wearing a classic plum jersey evening gown, fell for handsome "Mike"—shy and soft-spoken, with gorgeous wide-set blue eyes. But Mike, just twenty-four, was needy—needing people and needing to impress. They married in early 1937, and Mike's fondness for drinking soon took over their relationship. Before their marriage, the only time Mary drank heavily was in the immediate aftermath of Ken's death; now she was drinking routinely. Emblematic of the role alcohol played in their lives, Mike built bars throughout the house so he wouldn't have to travel too far for his drinks.

Discovering God

Into this paradigm was born their son, Anthony "Tono" del Campo, on June 5, 1939. He would be baptized Catholic—no ifs, ands, or buts—out of which flowed a friendship with his godparents, Bill and Mary Gargan. One weekend at their Palm Springs retreat, Mary began asking about the Catholic faith. She was curious.

By that time, she writes, "I knew what it was like to live the 'glamourous' life of a Hollywood actress, to be married three times, and to have two children. I knew too the inner deadness that comes from a life lived without purpose other than self-pleasure and indulgence"—always looking for "someone to lean on."[30]

Her host suggested she talk with Fr. Augustin O'Dea, who could answer all her questions. Assuring her not all priests were like a spider in a web waiting to nab their prey, he casually suggested a few books, which she devoured, soon returning them to Nazareth House in the Valley—where he directed wayward boys—and leaving with a whole new batch.

On her next visit to Palm Springs, she attended her first mass with the Gargans. Then, in December 1940, Bette Davis asked her to costar in *The Great Lie*, which became her sole focus for a time.

But when Mike announced it was his duty as a British subject to enlist with the Royal Canadian Air Force, Mary, knowing he would be leaving for good, renewed her conversations with Fr. O'Dea and began attending Mass at St. Monica's, closer to home.

Since her checkered life had been cruelly splattered in the worldwide press, one concept she found particularly powerful was God as a loving Father. But she was unclear about sin and badgered Fr. O'Dea for more answers. He told her to stay calm; faith was a gift that would come in its own time. Meantime, she must petition God for it. So Mary began praying the rosary, though the meditations on the mysteries were too deep for her. So she began saying a novena to St. Therese of Lisieux, with a prayer for light and faith, which she had picked up in the church vestibule. One night, when she opened a little porcelain snuffbox where she kept her rosary, she smelled roses. Mike teased her about it, asking if she had been praying to St. Thérèse.[31] Father O'Dea, too, downplayed it. But in her mind, there was no doubt it was a miracle, prompting her to review all the truths of the faith with Fr. O'Dea.

Then, one morning, as she was reading a biography of St. Thérèse, tiring of it because it was too saccharine, she nonetheless continued and came upon the words, "Jesus Christ is God." "Those four words," she writes, "were a revelation which made me slip to my knees in prayer.... If Christ were God, and lived on this earth, then anything could happen. Even my tangled life could be untangled."[32] Accompanying this "illumination," she writes, was "an actual physical brilliance," that required her to close her eyes.[33]

Fr. O'Dea agreed she had been given "the gift of faith" and after she read more books, he said she was ready to be baptized.[34] First, though, she needed to sort through her marital situation, which was straightforward, he said: Ken had died. Her marriage to Franklyn Thorpe was invalid in the eyes of the Church. If she and Mike were ever to resume their life together, they would simply have to be married in the Church.

Nineteen-forty-one was "my year," she writes.[35] She converted to Catholicism; cemented her acting reputation with *The Great Lie*, for which she won an Oscar, and *The Maltese Falcon*; and began doing radio shows—*The Hollywood Showcase*, followed by *Lux* and *Screen Guild*. To top it off, she had learned to fly—making her first solo flight the day Japan attacked Pearl Harbor!

Counting on Her Own Strength
As the difficulties mounted, though, her faith waned. But for "the unseen and unfailing ministrations of this Tremendous Lover," she writes, she would have been utterly destroyed.[36]

Nineteen-forty-three was not her year. That year, she signed with Metro Goldwyn Mayer, and, to her increasing dismay, began playing mother roles almost exclusively—same voice, same look, same attitude. Then, on February 3, her father died, leaving her with the burden of caring for her often demanding mother. The next several years were not particularly good, either. On December 24, 1945, she got married for her fourth and final time to Thomas "Tommy" Gordon Wheelock, an unsuccessful businessman and retired Army sergeant. He had decided she was the one for him. He wasn't—especially given his fondness for alcohol and lack of resources.

On January 18, 1947, her mother, Helen, died. Mary inherited her diary, and as she read the devastating narrative, she turned to alcohol to mask the pain. During a much-needed vacation with Tommy at the beautiful estate of her friend, Bobsey, on the Chesapeake in Chesterton, Maryland, she went fishing on their hosts' cabin cruiser and drank too much. Her alcohol-induced downward spiral was just beginning.

While entertaining a doctor one night back home in L.A., Mary, though drinking little, suddenly felt dizzy and disoriented. The doctor took one look and realized she was ill. Her temperature was 105. Later, at Queen of Angels Hospital, she was diagnosed with cirrhosis of the liver and told to quit drinking. Following doctor's orders, three months later, her excellent results lifted the prohibition, and she began drinking with abandon. Mary politely declined an intervention offered by a friend of Tommy's. She had just signed a long-term contract with MGM in 1946, which promised retirement in ten years, at age fifty, with a good annuity, and she knew how to stop drinking when necessary. But after making *Claudia and David* (1946) for Twentieth Century Fox; *Cynthia, Cass Timberlane*, and *Desert Fury* for Paramount in 1947; and finally *Little Women* (1949) for MGM—she was ready to explode. She had supported everyone all her life—her parents, her children, now her husband—and needed out.

Released from her MGM contract, she began occasionally shutting herself up in the library to sleep and drink, when not painting or parenting. Painting was a great diversion; parenting a nonstop job. Soon finding herself in a constant "drunk-sober" state, she finally entered a sanitarium.[37] There, in God's marvelous Providence, she writes, the psychiatrist gave her books to read, one of which was Thomas Merton's *The Seven Storey Mountain*, which opened her eyes to her need for God. She resolved to "never again take my hand from His." No more wild escapes! "I would walk humbly and carefully with Him."[38]

Counting on God's Strength

This time, turning to the Church wasn't just an emotional response. "I had confidence only in God. I knew my weaknesses."[39]

To strengthen her faith, she turned to Archbishop Fulton J. Sheen's recent *Peace of Soul*, Fr. John A. O'Brien's *The Road to Damascus*, Thomas à Kempis's *The Imitation of Christ*, and St. Francis de Sales's *Introduction to the Devout Life*, among other books. She also dusted off her rosary and began attending Mass again. Yet, her marital situation still prevented her from receiving the sacraments. While making decisions relative to her children's schooling, all was being put in order, she writes—all but herself. She spent practically the entire year of 1949, in bed—her knees, elbow, shoulder, and jaw throbbing with neuritis.

By 1950, her daughter, Marylyn, was busting to finish her studies and become a Catholic.[40] Meanwhile, Mary would make the occasional social call to Fr. O'Dea and share her difficulties with Tommy, and she would also discuss her steadfast conviction that receiving the Sacraments would remove "the burden of guilt."[41] Fr. O'Dea had a solution. Since she and Tommy had not lived as man and wife for a year, all Tommy needed to do was sign a paper agreeing to maintain the status quo. He would submit it to the Chancery with a note, stating their complex financial situation prevented them from divorcing at the present time. Tommy agreed and Fr. O'Dea promptly came over to Mary's house; she was too ill to walk or get out of bed. He heard her confession and gave her absolution and "with tears in his voice (said) 'Welcome home, Mary.'"[42]

Falling and Getting Back Up

After that, Mary stopped moping around and started going to Mass again. She also went to a doctor and began improving physically. Then life became hectic. As Tommy was pursuing a new business deal, Marylyn gave birth to her first child. Mary's nerves were shot and the doctor prescribed sleeping pills—crutches that failed to provide good rest or get to the root of her tension and resulting insomnia.

On May 10, 1951, as she tried to relax while Tommy was out, she spied some Vodka and began drinking. "The rest of that horrible night," she writes, "I recall only in disjointed fragments." After she accidentally took too many sleeping pills, she called Fr. O'Dea to say she'd taken some poison. The ambulance rushed to her home and, once at the hospital, they pumped out her stomach. The next day the newspapers blared, "Attempted Suicide." She regained consciousness two days later at Culver City Hospital and spent months recuperating.[43]

Upon her return, she began to cook and clean for herself and continued to attend Sunday Mass and go to confession, making sure her son received the sacraments, too. The peace and content-ment she felt after receiving Communion was not emotion or imagination, but a clarifying "illumination, a great relief from" the unrelenting pressure she felt. She would also say the rosary in the afternoons with great devotion and "sometimes," she writes, "I remained for long moments afterward on my knees, my head and arms on the bed, loath to break the precious sense of stillness."[44]

That July, she made a five-day retreat at Holy Spirit Retreat House, returning refreshed and beautiful, to Tommy's surprise. But by 1952, their relationship had disintegrated into "a morass of bickering and wrangling," she writes, as she coped with the inevi-table descent to its "complete disintegration."[45] At the same time, she took a home study doctrine course from Woodstock College in Maryland as she prepared for the Sacrament of Confirmation, which she received with Marylyn. She was knitted into parish life through the Altar Society at St. Cyril's. Meanwhile, the Motion

Picture Relief Fund shored up her faltering finances. Then, Menifee Johnstone, her maid of honor when she married Ken, got her a part in *The Grace Moore Story*; albeit filming would not commence until December.

Sensing the home atmosphere was bad for her son, Mary finally asked for a divorce one night when Tommy arrived home late—yet again. As the year ended, she was beginning work, while putting off the bill collectors, confident things could not get worse. Only they could.

As she was doing the wash just before Christmas, wearing rubber-soled shoes, she slipped on some wet steps and broke the fibula in her left leg. Too sick to work, in early January 1953, seemingly suffering bronchitis, she was taken to the Motion Picture Relief Hospital and was diagnosed with bronchial *pneumonia*. No wonder she felt dizzy and nauseous. Six weeks later, all recovered, the doctors removed her cast, revealing a left leg that looked "like a broomstick."[46] While feeling better, before her discharge, the doctor urged her to have a biopsy of her uterus. It was filled with fibroids—necessitating a hysterectomy in case they were cancerous. The fibroids were so widespread, she would have shortly died but for this intervention.

While recuperating at the Motion Picture Relief Home, she finally decided to read, rest, and relax. It was time. The priest from nearby St. Mel's brought her daily Communion, and she was able to make a calm, focused thanksgiving. Tono was being well-cared for and the Motion Picture Relief Fund was paying all the bills. She was feeling stronger. Back home, however, she realized she was actually quite weak.

It was early 1953. She was forty-six; her Hollywood career was over.

Feeling desperate, she made a novena to Our Lady of Perpetual Help at St. Cyril's, after which she got an offer, via Famous Artists Agency, to replace Shirley Booth on Broadway in *The Time of the Cuckoo* over the summer—one thousand dollars a week—which she eagerly accepted. But how would she get to the East Coast? Flat broke, she prayed to Our Lady for just the right words, and the man at Bank of America gave her two hundred dollars, after which she crossed the street to the historic Roosevelt Hotel, where she bought a one-way ticket to Washington and her friend Bobsey's hospitality.

On the Road...to Recovery

Shirley Booth was a tough act to follow, and the show closed early. But that experience got her another theater gig, from which flowed another. And, while she had been in near collapse and death in 1953, she gradually dug herself out of the hole. In 1955, she finally divorced Tommy.

In 1956, her new beau, Ferris Hall, proposed to her. While she had endured his impossible antics and drunken benders—from her arrival in New York through her two years on the road—she was fond of him and, on her way home from another show on the road, dreamed of accepting his proposal—only to discover he had gotten married three weeks before. (She had recently revealed to him that she had a heart condition.)

Crestfallen, she began drinking heavily again, drying out for ten days at Sierra Madre Lodge near Pasadena. The doctor, discovering her blood alcohol was quite low, attributed her condition to "secondary depletion." She was mentally exhausted. Deep inside, she knew she was lucky to be free of Ferris. And, though busy now filming, for the big and little screen, she had fallen into a "lonely depression." On winter nights, while the lone pine outside her window swung in the rain and the lonely dog cried out, she writes, "the self-pity would consume me."[47]

"Absorbed by [her] own nothingness," with only superficial connections to other people, her modus operandi had become "withdrawing, withdrawing; drinking to ease the unnamed pain."[48]

Television work, with its "piercing tautness" engendered in her one goal—the director's "thumbs up."[49] Each Friday, on the plane from New York back to L.A., she would begin drinking to relieve the loneliness 'hammering' away at her. "I still felt tense down to my toenails," she writes of one Friday's return—her shoulders and neck aching from the merciless pressure, "the mask" she didn't dare remove. On the way home, as usual, she asked the cab driver to stop by a liquor store.[50] By evening, stumbling, missing her *prie-dieu* kneeler and banging her knee on the floor, she pleaded in the words of the Memorare, "Remember, O most gracious Virgin...despise not my petitions, but mercifully hear and...O my mother, *answer me.*"[51]

Within weeks, after more TV and film work—this time followed by a days-long bender—she realized she was sick and "a sick person can get well."[52] She had stuck with her religion, she writes, because God "had never failed me [and]...I knew if I kept trying, I would somehow find the strength and understanding." She recalled someone telling her that "anything can be stood if it is understood."

But right now, she understood nothing. All she knew was alcohol, after it wore off would exaggerate a drinker's moods, and she was not a person whose moods were safely exaggerated.

It was Saturday, the summer of 1956. She had just turned fifty. It was time to confront her demons. She walked down from her flat in the Hollywood Hills on Highland, down to Sunset Boulevard, and turned left, down to Blessed Sacrament Church. No one was there. Undaunted, she went to another nearby church, where a priest referred her to Fr. Peter Ciklic, professor and chairman of the department of psychology at Loyola University in Manhattan Beach.

The next day, Sunday, she met with this "tall, fine-looking man, with a quick flash of a warming smile." To her surprise, he agreed to work with her. Alcoholism, he told her, was a symptom of a deeper problem and asked her to write an "auto-analysis" to help him analyze the forces underlying her drinking impulse.[53]

"Gradually," she writes, "the tangled threads began to form a pattern." She began understanding what had previously been opaque—namely that she had been abused as a child and, in response, had developed a pattern of escape, later taking the form of alcoholic binges.

After months of therapy, in the fall of 1956, she joyfully announced to Fr. Ciklic her plans to do another TV show in New York and then return through Chicago to see old friends.

He had his own announcement: "It has been a great joy to work with you, Mary," he said. "You were most wonderful and cooperative." She could call him any time, he said, relighting his pipe and blowing sweet-smelling smoke, but he was confident their discussions had revealed her "deepest conflicts" while she talked "without fear of punishment or censure." She had "worked through" her problems and "achieved a more effective personality adjustment."[54] Quite simply, she didn't need him anymore.

She had her doubts. But he reassured her, "Yes, Mary now you can walk alone—with God's help." After pointing out the "great self-knowledge," she had acquired, he said, "With self-insight you will continue to grow" and gain "self-acceptance and maturity."

Then, he handed back her stack of papers, suggesting she turn it into a book as a way of "making amends" to those she had let down by her "contradictory" behavior. She had achieved a "great release of tension" by admitting her "helplessness and defeat" to him—"one person"—which illuminated how much she depended on God.[55] But now she had to help others, which was also important to her cure.

Three years later, she gave the world *My Story: An Autobiography* (1959) in which she named the pain. With the grace of God, she understood it, and rather than letting it conquer and destroy her, she transformed it into a means of growth and sanctity. Now, her goal was not just pleasing the director, but the larger purpose of her life, namely pleasing Him.

The pain of growth, she realized, was much preferable to the pain of stunted growth. "I myself would have to do the walking. God would show me the way, but He would not carry me," she writes, "which takes struggle."[56]

She dedicated *My Story* to her parents "with love because [she understood] them now."

Five years after her autobiography was published, she made her last film, *Hush Hush Sweet Charlotte* (1964), costarring her friend, Bette Davis. In it, she played "a little old lady sitting on her veranda waiting to die."[57] A fitting swan song, she thought. After 109 films over forty-five years, she handed in her Screen Actors Guild card and pivoted to writing.

Life on Film, her final work, revealing film's "Golden Age," was published in 1967. In between her two autobiographies, she wrote six novels—*The Incredible Charlie Carewe* (1963), *The*

O'Connors (1964), *Goodbye Darling, Be Happy* (1965), *The Image of Kate* (1966), and *A Place Called Saturday* (1968), the latter about a woman who has an abortion and struggles with the aftermath.

On September 4, 1971, she moved into the Motion Picture Country House in Woodland Hills, California, where she had convalesced eighteen years earlier. She left it on May 15, 1972, and spent time in Mexico, said her daughter, Marylyn.[58] Exactly two years later, she moved back to what was now called the "Motion Picture Country House and Lodge," where she remained until March 22, 1984, when, records suggest, she entered their hospital wing.

She did not talk much about the faith, said Marylyn, who knew "very little about her conversion," noting her mother was "a very private person." But her daughter did remember her devotion to Mary. "I know she always said her rosary," which she kept draped over her lampshade. And she stayed in touch with the Gargans.

"As she grew older, she could no longer attend church," Marylyn said, adding, "It always meant something in her heart. I don't think she ever left it in her heart."

Fr. Padraic Loftus, pastor of St. Mel's, from 1974 to 1980, remembers her attending Mass at the John Ford Chapel, donated by the famed director. He also recalled giving her the last rites in the late 1970s as her ailments intensified and continued.

Mary Astor died on September 25, 1987, of pulmonary emphysema at age eighty-one—finally escaping into the loving arms of God.

Chapter Six
• • •

JOHN WAYNE'S
LONGEST JOURNEY
• • •

At the very end of *Chisum* (1970), Pepper says, "There's an old saying, Miss Sally, there's no law west of Dodge and no God west of the Pecos. Right, Mr. Chisum." And Duke says, "Wrong, Mr. Pepper. Because no matter where people go, sooner or later there is the law and sooner or later they find God's already been there." I think that sums up how he felt.

— A.J. FENADY, *CHISUM* WRITER AND PRODUCER

In the waning days of John Wayne's life, Maureen O'Hara made an impassioned plea for him to receive the Congressional Gold Medal.

"John Wayne *is* the United States of America," she told the U.S. Congress. This man's man—a hardworking, hard-drinking, heavy-smoking, chess playing, cussing, short-tempered lover of beautiful women—came to epitomize, like no other, American independence, courage, strength and heroism in a film career spanning fifty years and 185 films. His morale-building impact was such that he even helped win World War II with *Flying Tigers* (1942) and *The Fighting Seabees* (1944).

Congress honored him with that distinguished gold medal on May 26, 1979—his seventy-second birthday. The drama did not stop there. Fifteen days later—as he prepared to slip from the bonds of earth—he won the ultimate gold, arming himself, not with a Winchester but with the sacramental grace of baptism and extreme unction—storming heaven in true Wayne fashion.

An Anxious Childhood

John Wayne was born Marion Robert Morrison on May 26, 1907, in Winterset, Iowa—thirty-five miles southwest of Des Moines, and ten times as far from Chicago, due west.[1] There in Winterset, ice cream sodas were fifteen cents, groceries were delivered promptly, and the bells of the nearby Methodist, Baptist, and Catholic churches had distinct sounds (light, deep, and tolling).

It was America's heartland, and it was idyllic—except for the fact that Marion's parents, Clyde and Mary, born in 1884 and 1885, respectively, did not get along. Marion grew anxious as he witnessed his kind, likable father, a failing pharmacist with a heart condition and taste for alcohol, constantly henpecked by his mother, a stern woman, who kept a running tally of grievances, openly favored his younger brother.

After hop-scotching Iowa for greener pastures, the family decamped to Palmdale, California, in 1914 where Clyde's father owned eighty acres in the Mojave Desert, the last of the "frontier"— its fertile parcels long gone. Reaping predictably paltry harvests, the Morrisons barely eked out a living. "Mostly we ate potatoes or beans in one form or another," said Duke. "One Halloween, Mom gave us a big treat—frankfurters."[2] Young Marion rode a horse named Jenny to the grammar school in Lancaster eight miles away. When the horse became ill, he walked to school. He also stopped by the grocery store twice weekly. Once, after taking advantage of a special on tuna fish, the family ate it for months, which soured him on tuna for life.

In 1916, when the family moved to Glendale, Marion was

inseparable from the family dog, an Airedale named Big Duke, and would bring him to the firehouse. The firemen—real life heroes, whom the youngster idolized—befriended him and started calling him Little Duke. The name was shortened to Duke. As Duke writes, "My dog Duke and I were such pals that people started calling me Duke."[3] Thus was he rid of his feminine-sounding name for which he was ostracized growing up.

Duke Discovers Film...and Love

By 1917, Duke was attending intermediate school, getting good grades, paving the way for success in high school where he excelled academically, socially, and athletically. But life at home was increasingly chaotic—his parents separating in 1921—and he found relief at the local movie theatre. There he would soak in the movies of Tom Mix, William S. Hart, and other Western stars bursting onto the screen at the height of the silent film era.

Sometimes he was even offered the opportunity to help out the motion picture crews filming in Glendale, but it was just a pastime and in 1925, Duke landed a college football scholarship at the University of Southern California (USC), intent on studying law. In his continuing quest for a substitute father, he idolized his coach, Howard Jones, who was everything Clyde wasn't.

In the spring of 1926, he met Josephine Saenz, a devout Catholic, after a blind date with her sister, Carmen, while he was in Newport surfing. He soon began dreaming of this beautiful woman he would marry.

Around the same time, Jones got Duke and his college buddies a job at Fox studios. Mix, who owed Jones a favor, gave Duke his first lesson in the harsh realities of celebrity when, after being initially friendly, he brushed him off. Earlier that year, Duke had doubled for Francis X. Bushman in MGM's *Brown of Harvard*

(1926). Later that summer he worked as a Scotsman extra on *Annie Laurie* (1926) starring Lillian Gish. Lucky for him he was getting all this film experience, for a shoulder injury convinced Jones to cut him from the team. Without free meals and tuition, he was forced to leave school sophomore year and go work for the studios. Once again, Coach Jones helped him land work at Fox, this time as a stagehand, which Duke enjoyed so much, he scratched the idea of becoming a lawyer. Rising Fox director John Ford, fresh off his box office hit, *The Iron Horse* (1924), could not help noticing Duke and gave him some small roles in his films, even as he continued doing stagehand work.

Meanwhile he was dating Josie, whose calming influence helped ease his transition to film. But her socially prominent father— owner of pharmacies, who served in Los Angeles as consul for Haiti, Panama, the Dominican Republic, and El Salvador—was appalled at Duke's humble background, paltry career prospects, and split parents, who would finally divorce in 1930.[4] He was convinced the budding romance must be stopped.

"It was a great love story," said John Wayne's daughter-in-law, Gretchen Wayne.[5] Duke once stowed away in a ship to Hawaii, she said, just so he could be with Josie surreptitiously. He was caught and arrested, and afterward, his football teammate's father, a San Francisco judge, sprung him from jail.

Meantime, he was getting some breaks in Hollywood, as well. In 1929, Raoul Walsh saw him carrying a table across the stage and thought his handsome naturalness was perfect for the lead in his next Fox film, *The Big Trail* (1930).

John Wayne: Rise and Fall, Work and Marriage
It was to be the first outdoor extravaganza of the sound era, utilizing hundreds of extras and the expansive American

southwest—filmed in both 35mm and 70mm Grandeur film that captured the breathtaking vistas. As for their new star, they christened him "John Wayne" and gave him billing every bit as big as the budget, topping two million dollars. But the film, released on October 2, 1930, as the Great Depression dawned, was a flop, and Duke bore the brunt of the failure. After starring in *Girls Demand Excitement* (1931), Fox dropped him.

Will Rogers, biggest star on the lot, told a demoralized Wayne, "You're working, aren't you? Just keep working."[6] Wayne never forgot that advice and, all through his life, he would choose a bad film over sitting around waiting for the perfect film.

He next landed a six-month contract with Columbia but, as with Fox, was dropped—and was blackballed because Harry Cohn said he was intruding on his romantic turf, which was a lie, Wayne told biographer Scott Eyman.[7] Following Rogers's advice, he accepted work with other "Poverty Row" studios and began acting in poorly-paid Mascot films with equally poor production values.

But, God was smiling down, when, in the summer of 1932, Duke inked a deal with Leon Schlesinger. With ties to Warner Bros., Schlesinger made better films that paid more. It was enough to convince Josie that Duke was financially stable and, that December, she accepted his proposal, announced in *The New York Times* with twelve lines, Wayne getting "second billing."[8]

The couple wed on June 24, 1933, and settled down to married life and years of B movies at other Poverty Row studios including Monogram, Lone Star, and then, starting mid-decade, Republic Productions. Though typecast, he was working.

By mid-decade, he was also playing poker again with his friend, Ford—another strong father figure—on the director's boat or in all-night games at Ford's home. Naturally, Duke wondered if Ford would ever cast him in another picture. The curmudgeonly director held his cards close to his chest while Duke got valuable training and experience. He needed to wait till he was ready, Ford told his protégé. As his acting coach and friend, Paul Fix, said, "Duke was not...a natural actor." But, "he mastered one of the hardest things of all—to act natural"—so natural, he said, that most people didn't know he was, in fact, acting.[9]

The Western had receded in popularity in a decade featuring swank indoor scenes. But shortly after Duke's father died of a heart attack on March 4, 1937, Ford bought the rights to "The Stage of Lordsburg," a short story in *Collier's*, and a year later, gave Duke the draft script to *Stage Coach* (1939). Much to his surprise, Ford tapped him to play Ringo Kid in what would be Ford's first sound Western—fifteen years after his last silent Western. It was, as Eyman writes, "a model of concision and screen storytelling... [that] works off the deeply Fordian premise that Americans reveal their true and, mostly, their best selves under pressure."[10] Wayne soared in this, his breakout role—a performance Ford pulled out of him by his typically harsh prodding, for instance, grabbing his chin to impress upon him that you don't use it to act.

Fame, Family, and Temptation

Building on this success, he created that distinct screen persona (the voice, walk, and overall demeanor). He was also building a family—now including Mike, Toni, Patrick, and Melinda, born in 1934, 1936, 1939, and 1940, respectively. Wayne adored his children, but to support them, he worked tirelessly, leaving little time for family life.

With success came temptation. While Josie was pregnant with Melinda, Wayne and his costar, Marlene Dietrich, in *Seven Sinners*

(1940), began an affair that lasted nearly two years, through *The Spoilers* (1942). "In 1942," writes Eyman, "Hollywood and the public came to the simultaneous realization that John Wayne was more than John Ford's protégé; he was a genuine leading man."[11] He also had feet of clay.

The adulation and affairs made for a tense marital situation. Father McCoy would come by and counsel him about straying, Duke asking for forgiveness and promising to amend his ways, if Josie would let it go. But no sooner would Fr. McCoy leave than she would begin harping on his affair. "That's when I knew the marriage was over," Wayne said.[12] Unlike his father, Duke was not about to play the henpecked husband, and he moved out.

Nor did it help repair their relationship when Duke's next squeeze, Espinoza "Chata" Baur, whom he met in Mexico in August 1941 while surveying a business investment, lacked discretion. The marriage finally collapsed, and in October 1943, though it went against her religious beliefs, Josie asked for a divorce. The developing storyline from the studio publicity department was: "Duke liked to raise hell; Josie liked to go to society parties in Pasadena. Wayne is not a tuxedo man...Duke is passionate; Josie is cold."[13]

Gretchen said the notion that they were incompatible socially and she lacked passion is false. What is true is Duke "had a wandering eye" and she could not abide his infidelity. "Wayne felt guilty about the divorce for the rest of his life," writes Eyman. "In later years, he would admit to his children he had made a terrible mistake: 'I destroyed my first marriage...I was a different man back then. I was much more selfish," he said.[14]

Shortly after the divorce was granted, Duke married Chata at Unity Presbyterian Church in Long Beach on January 17, 1946, which Ford boycotted, asking, "Why'd you have to marry that [promiscuous woman]?"[15] Chata's mother ran a brothel, and she drank and smoked, and just wanted to have fun, clueless that stardom required hard work, especially at a time when Hollywood was facing stiff competition from the new medium of television. The marriage was doomed from the start and, by the late forties, Duke was losing his hair, his weight was down to 170 pounds, and he developed an ulcer.

Meanwhile, he was gradually being brought into the fight against atheistic communism and, while initially not wanting to alienate friends, finally agreed to serve in 1949, for a period of time, as president of the "Motion Picture Alliance for the Preservation of American Ideals."

By 1951, Duke and Chata's problems came to a head in Acapulco when Duke "threw a glass of water in her face. She responded with a bucket of water, he with a bottle of rubbing alcohol." One time, he said, she "passed out on the beach after a midnight swim and had to be carried to a nearby café, where she spent the night on the floor covered by a tablecloth."[16] He had also discovered Chata was having an affair with Nicky Hilton, the hotel chain heir. The couple separated in December—the same month Wayne bid farewell to Republic Productions.

Duke couldn't even find love from his now remarried mother, Molly Morrison Preen, who, complained about an all-expense world trip her son had feted her with in 1951, telling his shocked secretary, "I don't give a damn about him."[17]

Soaring Professionally, Righting His Ship Personally
The only love he found was in his work. Duke was at his peak professionally, making some of the best films of his career, *Fort Apache* (1948), *Red River* (1948), *She Wore a Yellow Ribbon*

(1949), *Sands of Iwo Jima* (1949), *Rio Grande* (1950) and *The Quiet Man* (1952).

"Brittles," writes Eyman of Wayne's character in *She Wore a Yellow Ribbon*, "represents the best part of the man playing him—a playful personality deeply attached to the earth, delighted at simple sights such as a herd of buffalo—a man more interested in preserving life than in taking it." Furthermore, the role exploited his "greatest gift as an actor: an ability to suggest an essential nobility of character between the lines and beneath rough manners."

Amidst his crumbling marriage, he met Pilar Palette in Argentina. It was while he was making his next film, *Trouble Along the Way* (1953), about a down-on-his-luck coach who saves a Catholic college. Wayne told his business manager she "was very attractive, very nice and 'very normal.'"[18] His manager sensed trouble. Sure enough, she became pregnant. Duke told her he would stand by her if she decided to have the child, no matter the career consequences, but she had an abortion. In December 1953, after the divorce with Chata was granted, they married and gradually welcomed three children over the next ten years: Aissa, John Ethan, and Marisa.

Wayne continued his grueling film schedule—now producing some of his films under his own production company, Batjac. He had to. He had financial commitments—not least of which, his two families. Not only that, but *The Alamo* (1960)—Duke's dream project, and directorial debut—was, in fact, his Alamo. During this difficult shoot, he was chain-smoking, and it failed miserably at the box office. Now, Duke needed to hunker down and do what he did best—act.

About this time, Duke met TV producer and writer A.J. Fenady, then working at Paramount on *The Rebel* TV series (1959–1961)

while Wayne was filming *Hatari!* (1962). Fenady had hired cutter (i.e., editor) Otho Lovering, who had worked on many Wayne films, including *Stagecoach* (1939) and, later, *McClintock* (1963).

One day, sitting in his office, as usual with his door open, Fenady said, "I hear Otho saying 'Hey Andy. There's someone out here who wants to come in and say hello. Is it OK?' I said, 'Bring him in, that's what doors are for.'"[19] So in comes skinny little Otho, and there "filling the whole damn doorway" is the Duke, who had come to take a look at the

Hondo *publicity photo courtesy Batjac Productions*

Hondo (1953) publicity photo with Lassie, Duke's favorite.

Both being Irish, they formed a fast friendship. "Duke introduced me to salsa," said Fenady. "He put it on everything—breakfast, lunch, dinner, whatever he had, he doused with salsa."— Commemorativo Tequila being the one exception.

Confronting His Mortality—Seeking God

In September 1964, Duke was diagnosed with lung cancer and had surgery to remove the upper lobe of his left lung. Filming on the *The Sons of Katie Elder* (1965) was being delayed, for an ankle injury, it was announced. By December, Duke went public with his ordeal—an ordeal which also included the private pain of yet another crumbling marriage. By 1966, Pilar and he were married in name only. She had grown weary of accompanying Duke on one film after another, the three children in tow. Still, he agreed to move from Encino, with its rolling hills and relaxing ranches, to Newport Beach to ease the tension.

Once he settled into life by the sea, he bought a yacht he named the Wild Goose. While reeling in the fish, the Divine Fisher was reeling him in.

He would frequent the Catholic Church on Balboa Island, where "he would meditate or contemplate and talk to God," Gretchen said. "And, he would take his cap off." Seeing this scene one day, the priest did a double take and walked down the aisle to check if it could, in fact, be "John Wayne."

"Yes, it's me, Father," Duke said.

God was smiling down on his bald head.

John Wayne with A.J. Fenady in Durango during filming of Chisum

He was soon cast in *True Grit*, in which he gave his Oscar-winning performance. The picture was released on June 11, 1969—exactly ten years to the day before he died.

His awakening spirituality was helping him channel his nervous energy into more than just making films.

"He was always a closet Catholic, I think," said Fenady, who while developing *Chisum* (1970), spent much time in many places with Duke during and between the filming of *Hellfighters* (1968), *True Grit*, and *The Undefeated* (1969). "He never talked [about it but] I know he went to Catholic mass down in Durango," Mexico—one of Duke's preferred filming locations. "That was one of the few times you'd ever see John Wayne on his knees," said Fenady.

Asked if he went with his wife, Fenady said, "He would go alone. He would go alone. He didn't want anyone with him. I know. He would go alone..." But he would not receive the sacraments, said Fenady.

He never officially became a Catholic, said Gretchen, because of his checkered marital record. Then, too, he was somewhat allergic to organized religion, referring to his coreligionists as "Presbygoddamterians." But the Catholic faith was different. He was "intellectually Catholic" and embraced it, initially, through what Gretchen called a "Baptism of Desire." He had a "real respect for the Catholic faith," she said, and he would talk with visiting priests into the wee hours about it.

All along, he was growing in sanctity, in his own way, evidenced by many acts of kindness and gratitude. Like in the thirties, when he stretched out filming one day while making another B-Western just so the extras could earn overtime money. Or in the sixties, when producer and friend Tom Kane's wife, Ruth, was at the Motion Picture House dying of cancer. One morning, her husband couldn't believe how great she sounded over the phone. "Well, how would you feel," she said, "if you woke up in the morning and John Wayne was standing by your bed?" Staying an hour, he brushed her hair before he left.[20] Another time, Duke invited this stranger onto the Wild Goose one day. He was the owner of a restaurant near Poverty Row, who had fed Duke gratis, after his career imploded some thirty-five years earlier. Duke never forgot his kindness.

When John Ford died on August 31, 1973, Wayne's heart practically broke, the tears gushing as he placed Ford's coffin in the hearse for the procession out to Holy Cross Cemetery in Culver City. That same year, Pilar and Duke formally separated.

Asked at the Harvard Lampoon forum in early 1974 if he "looked at himself as the fulfillment of the American ideal," he replied, "I look at myself as little as possible." Of course, he still commanded everyone else's attention. As his costar, Katharine Hepburn, from *Rooster Cogburn* (1975) writes in *TV Guide*:

From head to toe, he is all of a piece. Big head. Wide blue
eyes. Sandy hair. Rugged skin—lined by living and fun and
character. Not just by rotting away. A nose not too big, not
too small. Good teeth. A face alive with humor. Good humor,
I should say, and a sharp wit. Dangerous when roused. His
shoulders are broad—very. His chest massive—very.[21]

Still, as Eyman writes, "it was now clear that a hero who had
survived deep into a period devoted to antiheroes had finally been
tripped by time." The Western, which "perfectly accommodated
Wayne's particular gifts...was becoming extinct."[22]

Duke's last film *The Shootist* (1976) was about a dying cowboy
and mirrored real life as Wayne experienced coughing jags during
filming, his chest filling up with phlegm that needed to be force-
fully shaken loose by sharp jabs to his back.

After that, he was not well enough to make any more films,
which demoralized him greatly.

In April 1978, he had heart surgery at Massachusetts General
Hospital. While convalescing, a woman who prefers staying
anonymous gave him a St. Josemaria Escriva de Balaguer prayer
card. Duke took quite a shine to this saint, understandably so.
St. Josemaria taught that the path to heaven—to sanctity—for
someone in the middle of the world is through ordinary work
done well for love of God. If you boil Duke down, he was all
about hard work, done well.

His physical life, though, was not going well. In January 1979,
he was diagnosed with stomach cancer and admitted into UCLA
Medical Center that May, and suffered immensely.

On Sunday, June 10, Josie called him. Though it is unknown
what they discussed, later that day, Father Robert Curtis, a Paulist

priest, came to baptize and administer the other sacraments to Duke, including confession.

His son Patrick described this amazing development in an interview with Tony Medley.[23] While Duke was in a coma for ten days, Patrick said Fr. Curtis would visit and sit with his unresponsive father. On Saturday, June 9, he came to, while four of his seven children—Michael, Toni, Aissa, and Patrick—were visiting him. This man, whose children thought "indestructible," said Patrick, "was awake for two hours, talking and responding, and then went back to sleep."

"On Monday," said Patrick, "he was slowly getting worse." Then, Fr. Curtis called to say he wanted to visit. "Even though Dad was still in his coma, I said, 'Dad the chaplain wants to see you,' expecting no response. I started to leave the room when I heard him say, 'OK.' I was stunned." Patrick called Fr. Curtis, who arrived in 40 minutes. "With him still in a coma, I said, 'Dad, the chaplain is here,' and, once again, he said, 'OK.' I left them alone for 15 minutes and could hear them talking."[24]

Duke died at 5:23 P.M. on Monday, June 11, 1979.

Archbishop Marcos Gregorio McGrath of Panama, en route at the time of his death, presided at the 6 A.M. sunrise funeral mass at Our Lady Queen of Angels in Corona del Mar, held on Friday, June 15, attended only by family members. In the background, music from Wayne's movies played, including the theme from *The High and the Mighty* (1954).

Duke was interred on a hill overlooking the Pacific Ocean in an unmarked grave.

Josie died on June 24, 2003, seventy years to the day after her marriage to Duke.

A great love story, indeed.

Chapter Seven
. . .
ANN SOTHERN: SURVIVING
WITH OPTIMISM AND FAITH
. . .

I was so dumb. I never thought you stopped making money or grew old.[1]

— ANN SOTHERN

Ann Sothern was the very definition of a survivor. A diminutive woman, standing just five foot one, when she stepped before the camera or mike, bathed in lights, whether for film, TV, radio, or stage, she was ten feet tall. In a career spanning sixty years, she initially found fame and fortune as "Maisie" in the popular MGM film series (1939–1947) and played many other memorable roles, as well, including Flo Addams in Warner Bros.'s *Brother Orchid* (1940) about a gangster (Edward G. Robinson), running for his life, who finds sanctuary and solace in a monastery. Art imitating life, she, too, found solace in the Catholic faith when life delivered some tough blows.

Born to Play
Born Harriette Arlene Lake on January 22, 1909, in chilly but beautiful Valley City, North Dakota, her mother, Annette Yde-Lake, daughter of Dutch violinist Hans Nilson, and herself a concert singer and pianist, had gone into premature labor while on tour. Rushed to the nearest hospital, she gave birth to Harriette, while her husband, Walter J. Lake, was back home in Waterloo, Iowa, keeping the home, if not other fires burning. A meat salesman and

frustrated actor, this grandson of Simon Lake, inventor of the first submarine (the Argonaut) in 1897, was also a womanizer.

The family soon moved to Minneapolis, Minnesota, where her father worked as a produce broker and her mother continued her concert tours, when not teaching voice. Walter, who would often stray while Annette was away, deserted the family for a time when Harriet was four and her sister, Marion, two or three. He was a no-nonsense businessman, she a dreamer. After the couple's third daughter, Bonnie, was born in 1916, they separated, finally divorcing in 1927.

Harriette, who was growing into a redheaded beauty, sorely missed her father. In lieu of his nurturing presence, she received his financial support, which included her education at Minneapolis Central High and McPhail School of Music. Meanwhile, her maternal grandmother, Mrs. Nilson, provided emotional stability by watching over and teaching Harriette and her sisters needle-point, cooking, and life's wisdom as their mother toured.

Absent family harmony, Harriet found solace in the rich music her mother made—touring with her from a young age—as well as in her own music, whether playing violin, like her grandfather, or playing piano or singing, like her mother, who tutored her. By age six, she was performing with her sister, which included dancing, and ten years later, after applying herself steadfastly, she had developed into a lovely lyrical soprano and pianist, composing her own music. Named Minnesota's outstanding young composer, her "Study in B" was performed by the Minneapolis Symphony Orchestra, after which she was dispatched to Detroit to represent her state in a national contest.

Her mother's dreams of fame and fortune—if not person-ally, then certainly for her children—came one step closer when

Warner Bros. hired her in 1926 to be a vocal coach for stars transitioning from silent to talking pictures. But Harriette, who was just graduating from high school, decided to join her father in Seattle instead, where he ran a successful import-export company. Her choice of an academic path at the University of Washington, diverging from her mother's theatrical fantasies, pleased her father tremendously. However, a year in college convinced her to pursue the theatre after all, which caused an immediate estrangement from her father, who ceased all support.

She fled to Los Angeles, joining her mother and siblings, and landed a few dead-end parts in movies. By 1929, totally discouraged, she decided to head east for Broadway and was cast in Florenz Ziegfeld's "Smiles." She made her Broadway debut in 1930—but, only after the star, Marilyn Miller, uneasy with the sassy and talented twenty-year-old, got her fired in Boston, where she had auditioned. She was learning the cutthroat world of show business, and in 1931 landed the role of the ingénue in *Everybody's Welcome*, introducing the song "As Time Goes By," made famous in *Casablanca* (1941). After that, she had an off-Broadway shot at *Of Thee I Sing*—produced by the winning team of the George S. Kaufman, Morrie Ryskind, and Ira and George Gershwin. This led to another role on Broadway, where she replaced Fox star Lois Moran, whom F. Scott Fitzgerald had romanced.

It was a short road to Hollywood, where Columbia's Harry Cohn signed her and changed her name and her hair color. She was now platinum blonde Ann Sothern, cast in eighteen shallow but fun pictures from 1934 to 1936, including *Let's Fall in Love* (1933) and *The Hell Cat* (1934), plus two Eddie Cantor vehicles and *Folies-Bergère* (1935) with Maurice Chevelier. Next she signed with RKO Radio Pictures, making a string of lackluster films, which solidified her reputation as "Queen of the B's."

"Maisie," Fame, and Fortune

Then, the unexpected happened. Jean Harlow suddenly died on June 7, 1937, leaving MGM scrambling for a star for their planned series about a nervy Brooklyn burlesque dancer with a heart of gold, named Maisie Ravier—a character developed just for Harlow. At first they shelved the project just as Sothern went on a year's hiatus in 1938. Married to bandleader Roger Pryor, and living in rented luxury in Beverly Hills, she had had it. "'I found a much smaller house in Hollywood,' she recalled. 'We lived cautiously, not as extravagantly, for a year. I was just so sick of those pictures, I decided I wasn't going to do them anymore.'"[2]

When she reappeared in an MGM A-film, *Trade Winds* (1939), playing opposite Frederic March as a manipulative secretary— a role she would reprise many times—*Maisie* producer Walter Ruben refused to cast anyone but her in the role that would come to define her.

Playing Maisie Ravier in ten films from 1939 to 1947, her flawless portrayal of a character, whose can-do spirit was tailor-made for wartime and postwar America, prompted *Time* to call her "one of the smartest comediennes in the business."[3]

All the while, she begged MGM head Louis B. Mayer to let her drop Maisie. His reply was always concise: "No. Your movies pay for our mistakes."[4] But she did make *Brother Orchid* (1940) on loan to Warner Bros., alongside Edward G. Robinson, receiving second billing—before Humphrey Bogart. After that box-office hit, MGM began looking more intently for starring vehicles that would suit Sothern, including *DuBarry Was a Lady* (1943), for which Mayer paid $80,000 to purchase film rights to the

Broadway production. But Sothern rejected the revised script. So MGM offered it to Lucille Ball, Sothern's best friend in real life.

Another good friend was Muriel Weber, the wife of actor Ray Milland, whose marriage Sothern helped save. In 1987 she confided to *New York Times* reporter, Aljean Harmetz, her "secret" in this regard, "kept," he writes, "for more than 30 years. After Grace Kelly stole Mr. Milland from his wife during the filming of *Dial M For Murder* (1952), Ms. Sothern sent the actress an anonymous letter. 'I asked if she realized what she was doing breaking up the marriage of a wonderful woman, and I certified the letter so I knew it got there,' Ms. Sothern says. 'Not long afterward, their illicit romance came to a grinding halt.'"[5]

The lady had spunk. But that we know—evident by the way she played her cards in Hollywood. Yet, beneath that fiery, redhead temper, concealed by her bleached-blonde hair, there was added dimension in her life, inspiring that well-timed letter.

Peaks of Success and Valleys of Despair—Finding God
She had rather thought "Oscar" might be the next man in her life. She had divorced Pryor in 1942, after which she wed actor Robert Sterling, with whom she had her beloved daughter, Tisha Sterling, in 1944. But that marriage, too, ended in divorce in 1949, just as she was cast in a lead role for the first time in a big MGM A-picture, *A Letter to Three Wives* (1949).

By 1950, as her MGM contract was ending, as usual, she spent time in the winter skiing in Sun Valley. But this time she collapsed while spiriting down the slopes. The contaminated vaccine serum she had received while performing in England shortly after filming on *Letters* had wrapped, had given her a near-fatal case of hepatitis. Providentially, she learned of this ailment, which usually remains hidden until shortly before death, when she was diagnosed in February 1950 with a thyroid gland tumor. Though "a calcium deposit (pressed) on her vocal chords...her unfailing good nature won over all the hospital staff and visitors."[6] She was in hospitals on and off for a year, looking pale and yellow because of the hepatitis infection and feeling a nervous wreck because of the tumor. During her recuperation, which lasted nearly three years, she was only able to work on her *Maisie* radio show—and only when she felt strong enough. Gene Kelly and Audrey Totter filled in when she did not.

Her movie career was essentially over. While MGM was now a fading colossus—Clark Gable would soon be shown the door—she also had not been properly positioned when the lion roared to gain the leverage she needed to become an A-lister. As Oscar-winning Joseph Mankiewicz, who directed *A Letter to Three Wives*, said, "'Poor Annie. Annie was a damned good Broadway musical comedy actress.... But at Metro, poor Annie got stuck in the Sam Katz unit. She never got the big break Gene Kelly and others did, of being with the Arthur Freed steamroller of talent."[7]

Now without a career or a man and desperately ill, her friend, actor Richard Egan, a devout Catholic, started talking to her about faith. (He had earlier proposed to her, but she declined.) But more than words, the example his family set—large, warm and welcoming, strong and united in the Faith—deeply inspired her, particularly Richard's Jesuit priest brother. Then, too, her Catholic friends in Hollywood—including Irene Dunne, who was serene and calm; Loretta Young, strong and self-confident; and Rosalind Russell, possessed of a hidden, mystical power—helped win her over to the faith. The Coopers were also close friends. It all made a profound impact, and in 1952,[8] "raised like a weed," writes Aljean, "she became a Roman Catholic.... Religion got her through long months of lying on her back in the hospital with one-hundred-pound weights on her legs."[9]

Now, she had her man, only his name was Jesus, not Oscar.

After recovering, she made a big splash in TV with *Private Secretary*, starting in 1953, which aired for five seasons on CBS, earning her three Primetime Emmy nominations. That hit was followed by *The Ann Sothern Show*, starting in 1958, which aired for three seasons. She also made two more films in 1964—Gore Vidal's political satire, *The Best Man*, and *Lady in a Cage*, an Olivia de Havilland suspense film. In 1965, she played a mother who had been reincarnated as 1928 Porter automobile in the TV show, *My Mother the Car*, starring Jerry Van Dyke—the story-line a sign of the era's bizarre yet shifting tastes. It lasted just one season.

As the seventies dawned, like many stars in the post-studio era, her options dwindled to summer stock and dinner theater. As if that was not bad enough, in 1974, while performing in Jacksonville, Florida, flying scenery broke her back and smashed her legs, damaging the nerves. Gaffer's tape helped her make it through the show that night. The rest of her life was another matter.

She would never walk again, she was told. She said bully to that. Quite the athlete at her pinnacle—trap shooter, deep sea fisher, and skier for three months each winter in Idaho—after her accident she hobbled around with the help of a cane and put on the pounds. In 1984, she left Los Angeles for Ketchum, Idaho, not far from where she used to ski—a glorious view of Dollar Mountain brightening her spirits as she peered through her kitchen window each day.

She worked sporadically from then on. Her final film was *The Whales of August*, starring Bette Davis and Lillian Gish, which she made in 1987, just after her best friend, Lucille Ball, died. Her performance brought her only nod from Oscar—a Best Supporting Actress nomination.

As beaten up as she was physically, spiritually she soared—her sense of humor firmly intact. "I've done everything but play rodeos," she quipped after shooting wrapped.[10] "I don't want to own anything anymore," she said. "You reach a point when possessions possess you."[11] Her prized possessions, "condensed" in her living room, writes Harmetz, were "carved statues of saints, old photographs in gilt and silver frames, wooden crucifixes, porcelain figurines and an ebony piano."[12] On March 15, 2001, at age ninety-two, her heart failed, once and for all. As she passed from this valley of tears, she left behind everything to possess eternal happiness, unconstrained by a body, wearied by life's crosses. Crosses she had born so valiantly, that were now, happily, gone—eternally.

Chapter Eight

• • •

HOW JANE WYMAN
DEALT WITH TRAGEDY

• • •

She was certainly long on style, but she was much deeper and much longer in substance.

— FR. HOWARD LINCOLN

From early childhood, Jane Wyman adopted a quiet demeanor, prompting Marlene Dietrich, her costar in Alfred Hitchcock's *Stage Fright* (1950) to tell her to "get noticed."[1]

That she did, becoming one of the Golden Age's superstars in a career spanning six decades. In the process, she also became a superstar spiritually, gaining the strength of soul she needed to escape the Hollywood trap to which so many female stars, especially, have fallen prey. She almost didn't make it.

Traumatic Midwest Childhood

Born Sarah Jane Mayfield on January 5, 1917, in St. Joseph, Missouri, her father, Manning Jefferies Mayfield (1885–1922), was a cereal factory worker, her mother, Gladys Hope Christian (1891–1960), an office assistant and doctor's stenographer. Her parents were married barely five years when they divorced in October 1921. Rupturing her secure world further, a year later, her thirty-seven-year-old father, now living in San Francisco, died of a heart attack and her thirty-one-year-old mother moved to Cleveland, leaving Sarah with her older neighbors, Emma and

Richard Fulks. Mr. Fulks was chief of detectives. "I was raised with such strict discipline," Wyman later reflected, "that it was years before I could reason myself out of the bitterness I brought from my childhood."[2]

This emotionally spare upbringing impelled her to fix her sights firmly on glittering showbiz, where her talents flowed. Emma, sensing in Sarah a budding performer, took her to L.A. in 1928 after her husband's death, but the visit was short-lived. Back in Missouri by 1930, Sarah attended Lafayette High School and began a radio singing career as Jane Durrell. Not unlike other stars, she fudged on her age, saying she was sixteen not thirteen, so she could legally work as a "switchboard operator, waitress and manicurist."[3]

Hollywood Climb

In 1932 she dropped out of Lafayette and moved to Hollywood. There, she attended Los Angeles High School for a time while working at a local diner and auditioning—now with the help of Leroy Prinz, whose father taught her dancing in Missouri. Prinz got her a bit part in Busby Berkeley's *The Kid from Spain* (1932), after which she performed in a series of Fox and Paramount musicals as she began her slow climb to the top.

According to President Ronald Reagan's memoirist Edmund Morris, she married a young sales clerk named Ernest Eugene Wyman on April 8, 1933, shortly after turning sixteen. Though divorced by 1935, she kept his name.[4] At William Demarest's recommendation, Warner Bros. signed the newly minted star on May 6, 1936, as a "contract player" and, after a dozen or so films, she landed a starring role in *Public Wedding* (1937).

Ronald Reagan, the studio's other new star, a former Iowa sportscaster, was being paired with Susan Hayward. But "the suits" were looking for someone with a fresher Midwest persona and "Jane Wyman" was just right. Casting the duo in *Brother Rat* (1938), the official line was they met on the set in July 1938.

In fact, Jane had already spotted her handsome costar shortly after his arrival at Warner Bros. and, *Variety* reported, had a nervous breakdown on the eve of her marriage to Myron Futterman in late 1937, an allegedly wealthy New Orleans dress manufacturer. This brief, emotionally and financially draining union lasted just three months—putatively because Futterman did not want children. But, more than anything, Jane wanted "Ronnie." He was magical. "Marrying Ronnie," she said, "worked a miracle for me. It changed a dull, suspicious, anxious woman [into] someone at ease...I was drawn to him at once.... He was such a sunny person...genuinely and spontaneously *nice*."[5]

Getting him to the altar, though, took some doing. She was, after all, still separated, and Reagan would not think of dating a married woman. But once the divorce was granted, they began seeing each other, after which she watched him like a hawk. For instance, she made quite a fuss while on tour with "Louella Parsons and her Flying Stars" in late 1939 when Hayward would hit Reagan too hard in their act. Jane stood unmovable in the wings, seething if she got too friendly with her guy.

But that was nothing. As former First Lady Nancy Reagan told Morris, she threatened to "kill herself if he didn't marry her.... Ronnie, of course, didn't...want to marry, he was...much too young."[6] He enjoyed playing the field, squiring around the likes of Lana Turner and Ann Sothern.

"So she sent him a suicide note," Reagan continued, "and swallowed a whole, uh, lot of pills, and got herself taken to the hospital." Morris worked to validate this shocking story, and based on his research, it seems plausible. In addition to *Variety*'s nervous breakdown story, studio records revealed a memo dated October 4, 1939, indicating Wyman had been hospitalized for a "sudden 'stomach disorder.'" Digging further, Douglas Bell, Hollywood's oral historian "said he had heard Jane tried to kill herself over Reagan, but knew no details." Sam Marx (1902–1992), "the ultimate authority on pre-war Hollywood," had some contacts at the Los Angeles Police Department with relevant information. There were "no records of a medical emergency" involving Wyman, one cop said. Marx countered she became "violently ill just as she and Ronnie began to shoot *Brother Rat and a Baby* (1940). And they got engaged in the hospital." "Hollywood Receiving Hospital?" the cop asked. Marx said the memo didn't say and asked "Why?" Because, the cop said, "There was a young doctor there, known as 'stomach pumper to the stars.'" The studios, he said, were masters at keeping such stories under wraps. "Warners would have had several cops on the take, ready to go in and erase the records."[7]

Jane Wyman and Ronald Reagan wed on January 26, 1940, thirteen days after the *Brother Rat* sequel was released. As the decade unfolded, Jane's career soared, and Reagan became more interested in playing a real leader than acting one. "Jane used to tell me," her friend Ann Sheridan said, "that Ronnie was such a talker that he even made speeches in his sleep."[8]

Jane's performance in *The Lost Weekend* (1945) as the empathetic fiancée of an alcoholic writer was the turning point for her, leading to greater dramatic roles and her stunning Oscar-winning performance in *Johnny Belinda* (1948).

"I accept this very gratefully for keeping my mouth shut. I think I'll do it again," the thirty-two-year-old actress said, in the shortest Oscar acceptance speech on record. It was the very reserve she had developed as a child. But it was not shyness, rather a quiet, unrelenting drive.

Alexander Hall, who directed her in Frank Capra's *Here Comes the Groom* (1951),[9] costarring Bing Crosby, said "That gal can do anything she sets her mind to; she is one of the most creatively versatile performers the screen has ever boasted."[10]

And while her performance in *Johnny Belinda* is often cited as the pinnacle of her career for how she transformed herself into a deaf mute teen—a 'sound era' first—it was not her favorite film. This distinction goes to *The Blue Veil* (1951), her friend of thirty-five years Virginia Zamboni said.[11] Besides earning her another Best Actress Oscar nomination—for a total of four, also including *The Yearling* (1946) and *Magnificent Obsession* (1954)—it was a turning point in her conversion.

Finding God

After World War II, the Reagans hired a nanny from Roscommon County, Ireland, for their young children Maureen and Michael, her nephew Fr. Joseph Flynn told me.[1] Her name was Agnes Roddy, sister of Fr. Joe's mother, Kathleen. Agnes was a devout Catholic and, every morning, she slipped away to attend Holy Mass. One day, Jane finally asked her, "Where do you go every morning?" "I go to Mass," said Agnes. It made a deep impression. The Reagans were fond of Agnes, one year sending her nieces and nephews in Ireland a "red stuffed puppy dog," said Fr. Joe, along with a signed portrait of Ronald Reagan, then president of the Screen Actors Guild. Then, too, the Catholic community of 1940s and 1950s Hollywood was a vibrant one that included a whole constellation of stars like her friend Loretta Young, Claudette Colbert, Irene Dunne, Ethel Barrymore, Rosalind Russell, June Haver, Ricardo Montalban, Fred Astaire, Spencer Tracy, and many others. While acting in films together, the stars also typically attended the Church of the Good Shepherd in Beverly Hills and would meet up socially as well.

Wyman began attending Mass with Young at Good Shepherd in the wake of her divorce from Reagan by which time Agnes had left. She was nursing a deep wound over the loss of her baby Christina, who died on June 26, 1947, within hours of her premature birth. Exactly a year later, Reagan and she would divorce. As son Michael Reagan writes in his book, *Twice Adopted*, "It probably was the most painful experience of her life, and I don't think she ever truly recovered from it."[12]

The Blue Veil was coincidentally premised on the protagonist's loss of her newborn son. "Filmed in and around St. Patrick's Cathedral in New York City, *The Blue Veil* hit her in the face," said Zamboni. Everything she had learned about the Catholic faith from Agnes, Loretta, and others came into clear focus.

As Jane soaked in the spiritual grandeur of St. Patrick's during filming, she began to understand that her suffering had a deeper meaning and purpose in God's plan.

Three years later, on December 8, 1954, the feast of the Immaculate Conception, she was baptized, along with Michael and Maureen, at Good Shepherd by Fr. Francis Oberne, and received into the Catholic Church. Her godparents were Dr. John C. Sharpe and Sally Foster, Loretta Young's sister.

A month prior, on November 7, 1954, she divorced fourth husband Frederick M. "Fred" Karger, a Hollywood music director and composer, one year her junior, whom she had married in 1952. The interlocutory degree was granted on December 7, 1954, the day before she became a Catholic. Though the divorce was finalized in 1955, she remarried Karger in March 1961 and, exactly four years later, in March 1965, she was divorced again—"walked out on him," Karger told the Superior Court—and never remarried.[13]

But life was not one big cross. A savvy businesswoman, she moved to television with uncanny timing in 1955 as host of NBC's "Fireside Theatre," an anthology series, later renamed "The Jane Wyman Theatre." Her former husband, Ronald Reagan, was hosting a rival show for CBS, "General Electric Theater," during the same time frame.

Growing in Her Faith, Giving Generously

Fr. Howard Lincoln,[14] Pastor of Sacred Heart Church in Palm Desert, California, said Jane and he would "talk a bit about the forties and fifties and the great respect she had for the priests and the nuns" portrayed so flawlessly by Bing Crosby and Ingrid Bergman in *The Bells of St. Mary's* (1945). They were role models for her, filling a void in the absence of parental love and guidance. As Wyman grew in her faith, she became a Third Order Dominican, acquiring a gravitas that set her apart.

"She was the antithesis of *Sunset Boulevard* (1950) and Norma Desmond" Lincoln said. "When you went into her home," her Oscar, Emmy, and Golden Globe awards "were not prominently displayed in her living room," he said. Rather they were tucked away "in a little shelf in her den," essentially hid from view. That's not to infer that she was not "proud of her accomplishments as an actress," he said. She was. The point is, she was "not overstuffed with herself."

After she made her last film—*How to Commit Marriage* (1969) with Bob Hope—it was time for new challenges, said Zamboni. Jane met and befriended Zamboni in 1972 when she came in for treatment at the Foundation of St. John's Hospital and Health Center in Santa Monica, where Zamboni was an executive vice president.

Her main charity was the Arthritis Foundation, afflicted as she was with the painful condition, and, among other fundraisers, did their telethon each year.

She was also very generous with church charities including Hollywood's Covenant House and Our Lady of Angels Monastery, run by the Dominican nuns, Zamboni said. And she and Loretta "would always help me by offering their names and showing up at functions" benefiting St. John's and various churches.

Jane moved to Palm Springs in 1994 after closing out her TV career as Angela Channing in the long-running hit *Falcon Crest* (1981–1990), joining Loretta and Virginia, who had moved there in 1988 and 1993, respectively. Her charity work continued, the Arthritis Foundation transporting the entire telethon from L.A. to Palm Springs to accommodate the star, said Zamboni.

Jane was especially generous with Sacred Heart. "I had never seen a $100,000 check," Lincoln said, "until I saw one...signed by Jane Wyman" to finance cushioned pews, a state-of-the-art sound system, and a chapel for nearby seminarians.

Jane, Loretta, and Virginia became very close and would typically go to mass together on Saturday evening after which they would have dinner at a local restaurant, joined by Virginia's cousin Gabi.

Zamboni said Jane's faith "meant everything really, especially after Maureen died."

"A Holy Lady," Ready to Die
Her essence, said Zamboni, is "She was a lady." The lady knew how to stand up for herself. "She told me once," Lincoln said, "you know, in show business, you have to be tough." It was important, she said, to "stand up for your rights"—without losing your femininity. "She was tough in a moral way, an ethical way,"

said Lincoln, "in a business that is not known for its ethics and morality."

And, "She was not afraid to die," said Lincoln, because she knew her life would be "changed...infinitely for the better." One day, he said, "we're talking about dying and she's smoking cigarette after cigarette. Yet, by her bed" beside the ashtray "would also be a rosary and prayer books. So this was a holy lady."

The last year of her life, said Zamboni, Jane was not well enough to attend church, so they would bring communion to her. "She looked forward to this, even in the last month or so," said Zamboni. "Gabi would go over," and though she'd be dozing, "she'd always wake up and she could say all the prayers...whether she was with it or not."

Jane Wyman died at her home in Rancho Mirage early on the morning of September 10, 2007. She was ninety. Just as longtime caretakers Hans and Rosa were arriving, an emotional Zamboni said, she "gave them a wave" then "turned and died."

She was buried at Forest Lawn in Cathedral City, in a simple pine coffin, wearing the habit—about as far from the Hollywood glitz and the need to 'get noticed' as one could get. Now she was in God's loving arms. That's all the mattered.

Chapter Nine

• • •

SUSAN HAYWARD: FROM
BROOKLYN TO BOUNTIFUL

• • •

Only when I forgot to believe,
when I failed to trust, did I despair
and permit problems...to overcome
me.[1]

— SUSAN HAYWARD

Susan Hayward won her Best Actress Oscar for portraying unjustly accused and executed Barbara Graham in *I Want to Live!* (1958). She could relate—coming as she did from the same gritty world and possessed of the same volatile temperament, a product of both nurture and nature.

But unlike Graham, she was determined to overcome bruising poverty, debilitating handicap, and searing personal problems through hard work, chutzpa, and faith: "As long as you believe," her father always told her, "an angel sits on your shoulder and protects you."

"No problem seemed too big for me to meet, no day seemed without hope," she said—if she "believed."[2] But, as her problems mounted, she drifted from that childhood certitude only to rediscover her faith on the cusp of her Oscar-winning performance—in a clearer and surer way. God was there every step of the way. This she believed. To read her story, it's hard not to believe.

Brooklyn

Susan Hayward was born Edythe Marrenner on June 30, 1917, in her family's Church Street Brooklyn flat amidst a sea of tenements that housed poor Irish, German, Jewish, and Italian immigrants. The neighborhood, though close-knit and warm, was also dirty and foul smelling.

Her petite mother, Ellen Pearson, born on October 10, 1888, to financially secure Swedish immigrant parents, reeked of ambition and snobbery. Her father, Walter Marrenner, also slight of stature, was handsome but far less ambitious. Born around 1880, to parents of Irish and French Huguenot origins, he loved the theatre.

The couple wed on April 14, 1909, against both their parents' wishes—the Episcopalian Pearsons despising Walter's Catholicism; the Marrenners, fearing their son would lose his faith by marrying outside the church. Walter, with nervous green-gray flitting eyes, dabbled in theatrical jobs, but with children arriving—Florence in mid-1910, Walter Jr. (Wally) in late 1911—his domineering, taunting wife insisted on steady work, and he was hired as a guard at IRT (Interborough Rapid Transit), which became his life-long work—that and guiding Edythe, born six years after Wally.

Edythe, sensitive and shy, with a fiery temperament, idolized her father. "You must be like a rubber ball," he always said. "The harder they hit, the higher you'll bounce." One day, after a boy beat her up for borrowing his bike, he said, "Next time, you stay there and hit him back."[3]

Her mother maintained a façade of material comfort—keeping the apartment spic-and-span and showcasing a few elegant pieces. Birthday celebrations always included sixty-cent cakes from Ebinger's. But mostly theirs was a dreary existence replete with poverty's indignities, epitomized by frequent repossession of ovens bought on installment plans and Walter seeking relief in in the arms of his mistress.

They couldn't even afford to buy nearsighted Edythe a pair of glasses.

One bright summer day, shortly after her seventh birthday, as she was playing with her three-penny paper parachute, it flew away. Desperate to retrieve it, she dashed onto Church Street, onlookers screaming in horror as a car hit and nearly killed her. Unconscious and bleeding, her legs were shattered and hip dislocated. The doctor set her in a plaster-of-Paris cast, urging her parents to take her to King's Hospital for traction, which they ignored, thinking it was a charity mental ward. Instead, they jerry-rigged traction pulleys at home, leaving Edythe with one leg a half-inch shorter and a bad limp.

Months of recovery was just what the doctor ordered for this intense little girl, whose imagination soared as she read magazines and dreamed of becoming an actress, free of poverty. But there was no money for drama classes, let alone a suitable wardrobe—her favorite gray linen dress stained with chocolate for months and her worn shoes patched with cereal box cardboard she stuffed inside.

All this character-building—including merciless teasing at school and a heavy load of chores at home, her limp notwithstanding—while seemingly thwarting her ambitions, was, in fact, forming an actress.

The turning point came when, at age twelve, she was cast as Cinderella in a school play and emerged a talented actress. Using money earned from selling newspapers and discarded bottles and cans, she began going to movies and studying the stars' techniques.

In high school she chose heavier dramatic roles and devoured books on Sara Bernhardt, who had lost her leg yet continued acting. She also distinguished herself in local theatre, and upon graduating from Public School 181 in 1935, began making the rounds at casting offices, sashaying in with her swivel-hipped sexy walk, a cookie in her shoe. Winning a scholarship at Feagan Drama School instead, she set her sights on modeling—finally, finagling a meeting with agent Walter Thornton, who signed the redheaded, green-eyed beauty to model for magazine color print ads, selling top brands from cigarettes to soap.

Hollywood

When George Cukor spotted her in the *Saturday Evening Post* of October 30, 1937, featuring "The Merchant of Venus" and his top model, he asked her to test for Scarlett in *Gone with the Wind* (1939). Her father, now seriously ill, worried Hollywood would break her heart, but, discounting his fears, on November 18, 1937, she headed west on a sleek train with David O. Selznick, wife Irene, and Cukor, joined by Florence. But her December 6 screen test failed to impress Selznick, who suggested she return home. "I think I'll stay," she replied. "I like the oranges." But, unlike her sister, she refused to sleep with the studio bosses, making for a steeper climb.

Then, one Saturday, she accidentally crashed onto agent Benny Medford's front lawn while bicycling. *He* was impressed with her spunk and beauty. He quickly landed her a six-month gig at Warner Bros. as a "contract player" through talent executive Max Arnow, who christened her "Susan Hayward," and enrolled her in Warner Bros.'s Drama School along with Lana Turner and other leading lights.

In December 1937, she made her brief debut in *Hollywood Hotel* (1937)—the story of Hollywood gossip columnist Louella Parsons, who took a liking to Susan. After several more tiny roles, Warner Bros. gave her more screen time in *Girls on Probation* (1938). But ever-punctual Susan with the "distinctive Flatbush cadence"[4] ruffled feathers and her option was dropped. More significantly, her father died on March 16, 1938, from uremia and complications from arteriosclerosis. Her heart was breaking. But not her spirit. After enrolling in elocution lessons, she began watching *The Prisoner of Zenda* (1937), starring Ronald Coleman and Mary Astor, over and over, pronouncing the words in the theater just as they did. Sounding like a debutante, she mustered the courage to visit her acquaintance, Artie Jacobsen, Paramount's head of talent, who signed her for $250 a week—"$75 for your talent and an extra $175 for your nerve."[5]

After playing a supporting role in *Beau Geste* (1939), starring Gary Cooper, she was once again relegated to B-movie roles, only to be rescued by Louella Parsons, who asked her to join her "Flying Stars," a traveling holiday vaudeville show featuring Ronald Reagan, Jane Wyman, Henry Fonda and others. "Anyone here from Brooklyn?" she would ask, to the audience's delight.

She had another angel on her shoulder—her deceased father—but hardly anyone else. As biographer Christopher Anderson writes, "Susan seemed too direct, too humorless...uncomfortable around her fellow professionals" and had an icy demeanor that "rankled the others, none of whom realized that it was she who feared them—not the other way around."[6]

Her friend, producer Ewing Miles "Lucky" Brown, disagreed. "She was a really nice person," he said.[7] She also knew how to act, finally getting her big break on loan to Columbia in *Adam Had Four Sons* (1941). At third-billing, it was her biggest role to date, and most enjoyable, paired as she was with Ingrid Bergmann, a pro, who knew how tough Hollywood could be for women.

But her career stalled. So at a showcase for Paramount, executives at the Biltmore Hotel,[8] after being introduced by production head William Le Baron, unlike the others, she "marched center stage, planted her feet firmly in front of the footlights and asked, 'Wouldn't you fellows like to see me in pictures?'"[9]—finally asking after spirited applause, "Well, Mr. Le Baron, why aren't I in more pictures?" Producers darted uncomfortable stares, but her message was clear, which was not lost on Cecil B. DeMille. He cast her in *Reap the Wild Wind* (1942)—his seafaring answer to *Gone with the Wind*—where she had the chance to "show that [SOB] Selznick once and for all that [she was] a damn good actress."[10]

As World War II settled in, she made films to build morale, including *Star Spangled Rhythm* (1942), starring Betty Hutton, followed by a dud, *Jack London* (1943), on loan to United Artists. She also worked at the Hollywood Canteen, dancing the night away with visiting soldiers and sailors on their way to the Pacific. One evening she met twenty-nine-year-old Jess Barker, fresh off two Columbia pictures. Later, when he tried to kiss her, she slapped him across the face.

Signed to star in *Dark Waters* (1944), she lost the role to Merle Oberon. Learning it was Paramount production chief Buddy DeSylva's way of teaching her a lesson, she pleaded, "I never meant to be rude or snippy" and whipped out her glasses, saying "See—I'm just nearsighted.... Please don't do this cruel thing to me!"[11] But he did. That night, back at her seedy Hollywood apartment, as she collapsed in tears, her mother made her own impassioned plea: "Your father and I didn't agree on very much, dear" except for that axiom about the bouncing ball, which she repeated. "Remember after your accident, when the doctors said you'd never walk again?" she continued. "This man DeSylva is doing you a favor. Now you'll be a top star—not because somebody handed it to you, but because you did it all by yourself."

First, though, she would marry Jess Barker. Susan believed if a guy kissed her, she should marry him. If she consummated a relationship, she was practically married. She was, in fact, pregnant. They wed on July 23, 1944, in a brief ceremony at St. Thomas Episcopal Church in Los Angeles.

The ten-year marriage was a pitched battle during which Susan made twenty-three feature films, starring in most, while Jess made just nineteen, playing only minor roles. His sense of self-worth was shaken by Susan's success, including box office hit *Fighting Seabees* (1944), starring John Wayne, which gave her the widest exposure yet, with the reviewers focusing mostly on her.

After she gave birth to twin sons, Gregory and Timothy, on February 19, 1945, while to the outside world, theirs was a storybook marriage, she began getting that nagging feeling that Jess was like all the other guys she dated, jilting her after using her to advance professionally.

As World War II ended, her days with Paramount did too, and as the mother of twin boys, she was in no hurry to get back to work, especially when Jess was approached for a role in Walter Wanger's *Canyon Passage* (1946). But to her dismay, rather than fighting for it, he began begging her to audition for the female lead. Selznick was now jockeying for her, too. But she went with Wanger, telling Selznick when he kept her waiting for two hours, "You can take that paper and stick it up your ass."[12]

She was one tough lady with great instincts to boot. Wanger found her just the right part in *Smash-Up: The Story of a Woman* (1947), a roman-a-clef mirroring the life of Bing Crosby's alcoholic wife, for which Susan won her first Oscar nomination. As with all such roles about down and out women, she brought a lot of herself to her performance.

Meanwhile, Jess had not gotten that part in *Canyon Passage*—and on September 30, 1947, after making *The Saxon Charm* (1948), which dealt with the same marital problems she was confronting, Susan filed for divorce—relenting after Jess promised to try harder. Instead, the couple began coping by drinking no less than two Jack Daniels or rum and Cokes each evening. That on top of the sleeping pills she was now taking spelled trouble.

In early 1949, Fox's Darryl Zanuck agreed to buy out Susan's contract for $200,000. (A day later, DeSylva lost his perch at Paramount.) It was a good bet. "Susan is a rare combination of two elements," Zanuck said. "She's beautiful and she can act."[13]

My Foolish Heart (1949), a loan-out Goldwyn/RKO production, earned Susan her second Academy Award nomination. After that, she made eleven Fox films—including *With a Song in My Heart* (1952), in which she played injured USO performer Susan Fromann, garnering her third Academy Award nomination. On the promotional tour for the film, released April 4, 1952, she told students at her former high school: "Always keep your chin up and keep a happy heart. Young as you are, you have one. Try never to lose it."[14]

She needed all the heart she could get. Her marriage was crumbling. Susan was a workaholic; Jess would sleep till noon. Even a trip to Europe in early 1953, which she cut short, could not rescue the marriage.

The beginning of the end came on the night of July 16, 1953, after a round of cocktails. Susan suggested she was Jess's "meal ticket." One thing led to another, and an enraged Jess gave Susan a black eye among other telltale signs of their rough fight. A week later, on their ninth wedding anniversary, she announced her intention to file for a divorce. "Reconciliation seems highly unlikely," she said.[15] Divorce was the last thing she wanted, and she freely admitted she hadn't been perfect in the marriage. But she saw no other way. The divorce was finalized in August 1954 after a nasty public trial.

On September 16, 1954, while filming *Untamed*, billed as the South African *Gone with the Wind*, a fire broke out. Susan grabbed an extinguisher while all the men ran to safety. Where were the men, she would ask at Cannes in April 1956. Indeed, where were they?

While dating Richard Egan in October 1954, whom she met during filming of *Demetrius and the Gladiators* (1954), when she was an emotional wreck, they went to see the premiere of Judy Garland's *A Star Is Born*. Susan began sobbing so vigorously, given the parallels to her life, they needed to slip out early.[16]

On April 26, 1955, shortly after meeting with Jess to discuss the boys and in the wake of Howard Hughes' dumping her, she tried to commit suicide by downing two bottles of sleeping pills. She called her mother by rote at 3:15 A.M., and, slurring her words, assured her she would always be taken care of—repeating the exact words on page 61 of the script she was studying, circling them in red. Her mother, fearing the worst, quickly called for help, and with no time to spare, her daughter's life was saved.

A week later, on May 2, as scheduled, Susan checked in at MGM for dancing and voice lessons and soon began filming *I'll*

Cry Tomorrow (1955), about singer and alcoholic Lillian Roth. A smashing success and her proudest achievement, it brought her fourth Oscar nomination. Her personal life, though, now included the likes of Don Barry, who, one day in October 1955, invited her for a cup of coffee, and the two began an affair, prompting Marlene Dietrich to quip, "Zat Red Barry sure must make good coffee."

Heaven

Susan, now thirty-eight, realized she was becoming promiscuous—not in the usual Hollywood way, but far from the good girl she once was. And she was determined to amend her ways.

That December, she attended a Christmas party with Harvey Hestor, whom she had met while filming *I'd Climb the Highest Mountain* (1951) in Georgia. One fellow, who kept to himself, finally began talking to her. His name was Floyd Eaton Chalkley, a former FBI agent, turned used car dealer. Eaton, though previously married, was a Southern gentleman with all the right pedigree. Born on June 19, 1909, he pursued Susan assiduously through 1956, as she continued dating. Feeling more ebullient, she also had a private meeting with Jess to discuss their sons. Weeks later, she checked into the hospital for "surgery... to correct a minor ailment," exactly how abortions were cloaked in those days, biographer Beverly Linet writes.[17]

Whatever her sin, it seems God was shining down on Susan when, on February 8, 1957, she married Eaton in a civil ceremony in Phoenix, Arizona. Vowing "to be a full-time wife," she sold her California properties and moved to quiet Carrollton, Georgia, population ten thousand, where Eaton had bought a four-hundred-acre estate. The small Georgia town radiated "community"—something Susan had not experienced since her Brooklyn days.

The estate, with its white fences crisscrossing lush green grass with horses grazing in the hot Georgia sun, features a seventy-five-year-old red clapboard farmhouse. Farther inside was "Casa Chalkley," a single story home facing a crystalline fifteen-acre man-made lake, stocked with fish and surrounded by breezy pines. Inside, Georgia slate floors complemented tongue-and-groove log walls painted white, with an entrance hallway Susan transformed into an art gallery.

Susan could not have been happier. "I'm a naturally moody person," she said. "My nerves are very close to the surface.... [But, my husband is] so calm and patient and understanding that I'm on a more even keel now than ever before."[18]

Eaton was a devout Catholic, attended mass frequently, and as a major donor, was close to bishops and cardinals. Susan, a lapsed Episcopalian, was impressed by the strength he derived from his faith and began thinking about converting. During a visit to Rome in 1958, they had an audience with Pope John XXIII, who gave her a large black onyx crucifix.

"I don't miss Hollywood at all," she said. "Not even my psychiatrist."[19] (She was now sleeping without aid of sleeping pills.) Only the right film role, she said, could pry her loose from this paradise. Wanger found it—in the story of Barbara Graham. And, so, nine months after vowing to play only Mrs. Chalkley, Susan began filming *I Want to Live!* (1958). While on location, Eaton sent her a dozen yellow roses every day.

On April 14, 1958, shortly before the film's release, Susan's mother died of a massive heart attack while she was at her side. A year later, now with another angel on her shoulder, she finally won an Academy Award, prompting the film's director, Robert Wise, later known for *The Sound of Music* (1965), to comment, she was as "important" to film as Bernhardt was to theatre.[20]

She had reached the pinnacle and was content to return to her life in Georgia, soon building a church, Our Lady of Perpetual Help, with Eaton, across the street from their estate. They also bought a cattle ranch in Heflin, Alabama, and a home in Fort Lauderdale, where they went deep-sea fishing. That and so much more filled their days—including copious business pursuits, under the aegis of Carrolton Inc., such as the Atlanta Braves, an Atlanta football franchise—and a host of philanthropic works, which Eaton's faith inspired him to pursue.

That faith was tested in September 1964, when his only son Joseph died in a plane crash. Eaton began drinking more heavily to anesthetize his grief—racked by guilt for not being in his life enough. By early 1965, having suffered a liver infection in 1958, he was beset by "sick spells."[21]

In the fall of 1965, Susan, still making the occasional film (for a total of ten during her marriage to Eaton), accepted a role in *Anyone for Venice?*—released as *Hollywood Pot* (1966). It was being filmed in Rome, and the couple used the opportunity for a second honeymoon and to visit the pope again, this time Paul VI.

Susan was in seventh heaven. Then one day in mid-October, her husband woke up dangerously ill from hepatitis. He was initially infected during World War II though a blood transfusion and was now dying.

Early on the morning of January 9, 1966, as the end neared, Eaton expressed concern for Susan's soul and asked her to convert to Catholicism so they could be together in heaven. In tears, she told him she would. Dr. Leonard Erdman, who was watching their conversation, saw the shock envelop Susan's face, when at 7:55 A.M., he breathed his last. She locked herself in the bathroom, where she let out chilling screams for ten minutes, after which she calmly made funeral arrangements.

After her husband's death, she told her producer friend of twenty-five years, Martin Rackin, "I look to God for strength. I won't say how or when I found Him, but when I'm under pressure I rely on God."[22]

Susan began taking instructions from Fr. Daniel J. McGuire, whom Eaton had met in 1952 while McGuire, ordained in June 1950, was serving as an American secretary at the Jesuit headquarters in Rome.[23] Susan met him during their 1958 Rome visit. In the intervening years, Fr. McGuire had moved to Pittsburgh, where he was pastor at St. Peter and Paul Catholic Church, which was affiliated with the Jesuit Latin Boys' School.[24]

On June 29, 1966, Susan traveled to Pittsburgh incognito and was received into the Church the next day—her forty-ninth birthday—at St. Peter and Paul's, with a beautiful all-wood interior. One parishioner, recognizing her, called the press, and within an hour, a news bulletin had been sent via teletype around the world. "God bless her," said Fr. McGuire. "I baptized her into the Church." When he got calls, he said nothing, as Susan wanted it. He did, however, correct the false published reports that the Bishop of Pittsburgh was present the day she converted; he was not.

Meanwhile Susan continued grieving Eaton's death in Fort Lauderdale, living as a recluse—getting through the nights with many stiff drinks and fervent prayers. Against character, she would just sit on her boat, gazing at the beautiful blue sky. She sold the ranch in Alabama, the estate in Georgia—even the home in Florida. The memories were too painful. Her neighbor Eleanor Carson said, "She was really not a very friendly person—except on a one-on-one basis. But I think she had a spiritual nature, and seemed to be searching for this deeper thing in her."[25]

Finally, in 1967, she agreed to star in *Valley of the Dolls* (1967), replacing Judy Garland. It was Twentieth Century Fox's highest grossing film to date and her final film for Fox.

In the summer of 1968, while performing the lead in *Mame* at Caesar's Palace in Las Vegas, she refused to enlist a coach to save her voice, when, inevitably, it gave out—one of the worst decisions of her career. Then, too, she was trying to be careful with her money. As Susan confided to her brother, "If Eaton had lived a couple years longer, I'd have gone bankrupt."[26]

Through all her travails, she kept the crucifix Pope John XXIII had given her close by. On the night of August 9, 1969, engrossed in the tale of her *Valley of Dolls* costar Sharon Tate's tragic murder by Charles Manson, chain-smoking as usual, a lit cigarette caught fire. As she escaped her apartment, enveloped in flames, she grabbed the crucifix.

The fire woke her up, literally and figuratively. Now fifty-four, she was determined to end her period of mourning and start living again—as a full-time actress. Her resolve notwithstanding, as 1970s opened, she broke her arm fishing in the Bahamas and got pneumonia while on safari in Africa. Upon returning to Fort Lauderdale, she broke her ankle when a motorbike fell on it. She was also drinking heavily—Scotch, Beefeater martinis, and Bloody Marys, all to help her chronic insomnia. But she steered clear of drugs, lest she become addicted, telling Robert Osbourne years later, "Whatever I do, I do intensely."[27]

By 1971, she had had enough. Feeling "like a freak," she sold her Florida condominium and moved back to L.A., leasing a house behind the Beverly Hills Hotel, where she "could be just another freak among freaks."[28] In the early fall, she approached Norman Brokaw at the William Morris Agency, who got her work—this time on TV.

While doing prerelease publicity for *Say Goodbye, Maggie Cole* (1972), she told a *Boston Sunday Herald* reporter, who asked if she would ever marry again?—"If God wants it, the right man will come along again. If not, so be it."

That December, while visiting friends in Georgetown, she had a seizure, after which she checked into Georgetown University Hospital. A dye, injected to test her liver, induced more seizures, signaling a blockage in her brain. They begged her to have more tests but she demurred, thinking it was just nervous tension. In March 1973, however, after she suffered another seizure, while socializing with friends in L.A., she could no longer ignore the symptoms. Diagnosed with multiple brain tumors, she began losing weight and gradually suffered paralysis on one side, and, toward the end, the other. As if that was not bad enough, she was also suffering from lung cancer. In the midst of it all, she was invited to appear at the Forty-Sixth Annual Academy Awards.

On April 2, 1974, as she arrived at the Dorothy Chandler Pavilion, she was wearing her signature sable mink fur. Introduced as "a medical miracle," she wowed the audience in her Nolan Miller green chiffon gown, with Van Cleef diamond necklace, bracelet, and earrings. The doctor had injected her with Dilantin before she went on stage to avert seizures—Charlton Heston leading her to the podium, as she gripped his strong arm. She was such a hit, that they invited her again in 1975. But, as she confided to Nolan Miller, it was the last time the public would see her.

That night, she met fellow Brooklynite, Barbara Stanwyck, for the first time at the Getty Museum, who began comforting her with notes, as Susan had comforted her with flowers when she was sick.

In July, she traveled to Atlanta for exploratory surgery at Emory University, then convalesced in Fort Lauderdale. By late summer, she was confined to a wheelchair, wearing leg braces to keep her brittle bones from breaking.

In September, Eaton's friend, Father Joseph Brue, dropped by for a visit, and Susan used it as an opportunity for "a night on the town," a dozen American Beauty roses greeting her party as they arrived at the "Tower Club." The next morning, Fr. Brue gave her Holy Communion.

Meantime, Katharine Hepburn had become a friend, visiting her hilltop house overlooking Laurel Canyon, bringing her baskets of healthy food and freshly cut flowers—and, to Susan's delight, demanding she get well.

It was not to be. Barely able to swallow, she became unconscious on March 10—all the while her right hand held the crucifix Pope John XXIII had given her fifteen years earlier.

Susan died on March 14, 1975, at 2:25 P.M. and was buried at *Our Lady of Perpetual Help* in Carrollton, Georgia. She rests alongside Eaton, her engraved epitaph reading: "I am the resurrection and the life." Through faith, she knew in death her life had just begun.

Chapter Ten
• • •

LANA TURNER: FINDING GOD
AND SECURITY—WITHIN
• • •

I have come a long way since 1937.
I almost can't believe how far. I
think it's because I've been close to
God these last two years.[1]

—LANA TURNER

Lana Turner, famously discovered at a Hollywood soda fountain, experienced a dizzying rise, soon becoming MGM's biggest and most glamorous star.

Known for *The Postman Always Rings Twice* (1946), *The Bad and the Beautiful* (1952), and *Imitation of Life* (1959), in typical Lana fashion, she drank in Hollywood with zest—the jewels, the furs, the glamour, the fun—while suffering the crush of adoring fans. The fans were the least of her problems.

Easily charmed by the wrong suitors and hopelessly naïve about their motives, she kept falling into the same trap—embracing their fantasies of security and love only to find, again and again, her dreams dashed.

Then, one day, like Dorothy in *The Wizard of Oz*, she found what she most craved was very near—right within her soul.

Humble, Tragic Beginnings
"Julia Jean" Lana Turner was born in Wallace, Idaho, on February 8, 1921, to Mildred Frances Cowen, a sixteen-year-old Arkansan of Scottish, Irish, and English descent, who revered

her husband, John Virgil Turner. Nine years her senior, he had been awarded medals for valor in World War I. Hailing from Montgomery, Alabama, of Low Dutch heritage, he spoke with a thick southern accent and had an upbeat personality that complimented Mildred's reticence.

The couple met in 1919, when John, fresh out of the Army, was heading west to work the mines, passing through Picher, Oklahoma, where Mildred was accompanying her mine inspector father. While dining at a rooftop garden restaurant, John asked Mildred to dance, and shortly afterward the couple eloped. When John's start-up dry-cleaning business failed, he returned to mining. That and poker supported the family, eking out an existence by the railroad, where watching the trains became a favorite pastime.

One day, Mildred told little Julia, now adorned with beautiful auburn tresses, to "wave" and "blow a kiss" to a "lady in long white gloves" on a passing train, telling her she was her "real mother." "I screamed and kicked and pushed her away until she dragged me into the house," Lana writes. Consoling her daughter that "she'd only been teasing"—Mildred often wondered why she had made up this story.[2]

Julia remembered her father as a "delightful" man, whom she resembled—same "bright blue eyes and small nose" and same "broad shoulders and slim hips." "After sitting me on his lap he'd stand me on the floor and teach me how to tap-dance," she writes, showing her the steps he performed at the local Elks Club. "He could sing well, too," and "was alive with talent."[3]

Both of her parents were "handsome" and, though poor, dressed well, which shaped Julia's tastes. When she was four, she was so captivated by the pretty clothes her mother was modeling, that, she writes, "I put on a fur jacket and minced on stage, imitating her."[4]

When she was six, the family escaped to San Francisco and to keep the trip interesting, her parents conjured up spectacular images of the "Golden Gate." Upon arriving, seeing a wide expanse of water and no pearl covered shining gate, she balled her eyes out.

Penniless, the family settled in Stockton, and her father began cashing in on Prohibition by making "moonshine," which Julia blurted out at school one day. While John got off with a reprimand, he hit the road, this time alone, and the couple split—the two girls relocating to Sacramento, where Mildred worked in a beauty parlor and Julia attended Catholic school.

Initially they lived in a group house, where the women, bringing their men friends home at night, hid Julia in a large closet with a mattress, prompting Mildred to place her with a Stockton family—the "Hislops"—while she worked in San Francisco.

"On Sundays I went to the Catholic church with the Hislops," Lana writes. "The ritual thrilled me so that I wanted to convert, and my mother agreed." Originally christened Jean, she chose Frances for her saint's name—preceding it with "Mildred" in honor of her mother.[5]

Her father was "furious" about her conversion. He did, however, make sure his daughter's material desires were fulfilled.[6] One day, when they were shoe shopping, Julia picked out "patent leather pumps with little Cuban heels," which caused a fuss at home. It was the beginning of her shoe fetish, later requiring "a special room, with shelves from floor to ceiling, filled with shoes," she writes—"698 pairs."[7]

Another time, "I asked my father to buy me a bicycle and he promised that one day he would." Soon thereafter, Mildred brought Julia back to San Francisco. That night, she writes, "I

saw a huge medallion of shining gold, and on it was embossed
the face of God, a shimmering countenance, comforting, benign.
A voice said, 'Your father is dead.'" The next morning, he was
found murdered. He was buried at the Presidio with full military
honors.[9]

A few years later, she learned the real story of her father's demise
when she came across a news clip about a "traveling crap game"
he sometimes partook of. "On the night of December 14, 1930,"
the story reported, "the game was held in the basement of the *San
Francisco Chronicle* building." On a "winning streak," he said
"he planned to buy his little girl a bicycle," tucking his winnings
into his left sock. "The next morning," she writes, "they found
him slumped against a wall at Mariposa and Minnesota streets"
near Potrero Hill. "He had been bashed in the head with a black-
jack, and his left foot was bare."[10]

With her father gone, she endured another year at the Hislops'.
Her story there ended when one of the children beat her up, after
which her mother found lodgings for her with a large Italian
family in nearby Lodi before bringing her back to San Francisco
to live with her boss and her two young children.

While attending Presidio Junior High, Julia began going to the
matinees, scraping together the twenty-five-cent admission by
saving a nickel of lunch money each day. Getting her first taste of
the stars, she writes, "That was real entertainment." She particularly loved Kay Francis, who strongly resembled her mother, and
Norma Shearer, who was "so beautiful, so glamorous."

From Soda Fountain to Hollywood's Pinnacle

Legend has it that "Lana Turner" was discovered at Schwab's—a
rumor started by Hollywood columnist Sidney Skolskey when a
buxom blonde asked him which was the legendary star's stool.

He picked one out, making Schwab's the mecca for those hoping to repeat Lana's success. It was actually W.R. "Billy" Wilkerson, publisher of the *Hollywood Reporter* and friend of MGM boss Louis B. Mayer, who spotted her—at another soda fountain.

Julia and her mother had moved to Los Angeles in 1936, in the depths of the Great Depression, when her mother, having buffered Julia from the worst of the flailing economy, got sick and needed a warm climate to recover, and Mildred's friend in Los Angeles, Gladys Taylor, offered to take them in. It was a harrowing trip, their constantly chattering female driver once losing control of the car on a muddy road during a storm, causing it to flip over. "We rattled our way into Los Angeles—the biggest city I'd ever seen," Lana writes, "its wide streets lined with ornate stone buildings, with bright, imposing signs." The driver dropped them off at the corner of Sunset Boulevard and Highland Avenue. "That," she writes, "was my introduction to the movie capital of the world."[11]

After a month at Hollywood High, one day, cutting typing class, she skipped over to the "Top Hat Malt Shop" for a Coke. Wilkerson stared at her until he finally asked if she would like to be in the movies. "I don't know," she replied. "I'd have to ask my mother." So he gave her his card.[12]

Wilkerson sent Julia to talent agent Zeppo Marx, who had her introduced to various casting directors, none of whom could find the inexperienced teen any work—even as an extra. Finally, Solly Biano took her to Warner Bros. in Burbank, where all the casting director said was, "'Lift your skirt, walk and turn around.' Furious, embarrassed and trying not to cry," she writes, "I kept my eyes on the floor."[13]

Striking out with Biano, a determined Solly remembered that Mervyn LeRoy, known for *Little Caesar* (1931), was looking for a sixteen-year-old girl for his film *They Won't Forget* (1937), based on *Death in the Deep South*. Julia had just turned sixteen and Warner Bros. signed her, after which LeRoy transformed her into the sexually alluring object of desire that was her trademark—her scenes in *They Won't Forget* marked by what LeRoy called "flesh impact."[14]

A year later, LeRoy left Warner Bros. for MGM, bringing along his star, newly christened "Lana Turner," and shortly after her seventeenth birthday, MGM signed her. "I was not just a six-month option girl to be passed around the executive offices," she writes, but "LeRoy's protégé."[15] She was immediately cast in *Love Finds Andy Hardy* (1938), starring Mickey Rooney and Judy Garland and, when not working, attended MGM's "little red schoolhouse."

Being a bit older, she rebelled and would smoke in the bathroom. Likewise, when she went out, usually in large groups, she would ask for a drink, take a sip and leave it on the table. Drinking was one thing her mother forbade.[16]

In a sign she was getting noticed, MGM offered her the chance to appear in *Idiot's Delight* (1939), starring Clark Gable, in which he performed with a straw hat and cane, surrounded by four blondes. They bleached her hair blonde for the screen-test, and though she did not get the part, she remained a "golden blonde."[17]

With the coming of World War II, a new prosperity in the air, Lana began hanging with Linda Darnell, Bonita Granville, Ann Rutherford, Jackie Cooper, Mickey Rooney, and others.

"Believe it or not," she writes, "we never did anything naughty." The worst they did was "cruising"—piling into someone's convertible, the top down, and going to the drive-in, where they would see a group of boys in a car and begin flirting. If someone asked if she was "Lana Whatshername," she writes, "I'd say, 'Oh, no, I've been told I look like her,'" before screeching off.[18] While innocent enough, Mayer, getting wind of their antics, called Lana and her mother in, warning her, tearfully, to cool it. She was risking her career, he said, implying in a crude way she was only interested in sex.

Dreams Implode Amidst the Golden Age

By 1939, she had her first steady boyfriend, Greg Bautzer, a suave lawyer ten years her senior, dubbed "the man who seduced Hollywood," in the so-titled biography by B. James Gladstone. (Thirty years later, he would engineer Kirk Kerkorkian's MGM takeover.) "He seemed enchanted by my vivaciousness and lack of worldly wisdom," she writes, and "loved to show me off at the most glamorous places like Ciro's or the Trocadero." Her desire to appear older was the perfect bait, and he knew just how to reel in his prey—"seventeen, romantic and a Virgin"—and they soon "made love." What she didn't realize, she writes, is all the "action" he was getting "on the side." When Joan Crawford let her know he was hers, Bautzer denied the story and Lana grew more confused, spending agonizing evenings swinging from "love to hurt to rage to humiliation."[19]

To heal the wounds, she threw herself into her work—*These Glamour Girls* (1939) and *Dancing Co-Ed* (1939), featuring band leader Artie Shaw. Shaw began wooing her—one evening painting a romantic vision after which they precipitously wed in Vegas. When her mother asked her why she married him, she said, "Because I think I'm going to be happy." Within three days, she knew that was a false hope. Two months later she learned of the two previous Mrs. Shaws. He was mercurial and abusive—his "bullying, frightening displays" continuing, she writes, until one night she became "hysterical" and required emergency medical care and a hospital stay.[20] No sooner had she filed for divorce than she discovered she was pregnant. Her agent, Johnny Hyde, reminded her of MGM's strict taboo about having a baby, unmarried. "Reluctantly," she told him, "the answer was yes"—she wanted to remain at the studio. Toward this end, she went by herself to an "abortionist," who worked out of a "dirty, dingy private house downtown," she writes, and, who nearly killed her in the process of killing her baby.[21]

Once again, in 1940–1941, work rescued her. While filming *Ziegfield Girl* (1941), she writes, "I discovered how much I *liked* acting."[22] Her salary increasing to $1,500 a week, she made four more films that year, including *Dr. Jekyll and Mr. Hyde* (1941) with Spencer Tracy, *Honky Tonk* (1941) with Clark Gable, and *Johnny Eager* (1941) with Robert Taylor, who mistook on-screen flirtations, sometimes spilling off-screen, to a full-blown romance, damaging his marriage with Barbara Stanwyck, to Lana's regret.

Feeling wealthier, she bought a Moderne-style home in Westwood, where she hosted regular Sunday soirees, including the day the Japanese attacked Pearl Harbor. Partying with Tommy Dorsey, Frank Sinatra, Buddy Rich, and two of her "favorite girlfriends"—Linda Darnell and Susan Hayward—they did not realize until after her mother arrived back from a trip to San Francisco that the nation was at war.[23]

Along with other Hollywood stars, she was enlisted to whip up enthusiasm at bond rallies, where she promised a "sweet kiss" to any man in the crowd who bought a $50,000 bond, increasing the defense budget by several million. Her allure was, of course, legendary.

While making her next film, *Somewhere I'll Find You* (1942), again paired with Clark Gable, his wife, Carole Lombard, was killed in a plane crash. Anxious to get home, given her concern over Lana, though scheduled to return by train, she took that fateful flight instead, so "the dreadful rumor" went. About the same time, her brief romance with Howard Hughes ended when she finally concluded, with breathtaking understatement, "it wasn't my mind he was after."[24]

While making a war-bond swing through her hometown of Wallace, Idaho, she reflected how, only five years earlier she had walked down that studio back lot in her first film wearing that tight-fitting sweater. Fifteen films, one marriage, one divorce, and one abortion later, she had become "America's glamour queen."[25]

Something was clearly missing.

Back in L.A., she thought she knew what it was when she met Joseph Stephen Crane III at a studio party. He was in the tobacco business, he said, and given her "weakness for a certain kind of good looks, coupled with witty charm," she accepted his story. Within three weeks, he proposed and on July 17, 1942, she was off to Vegas, once again pledging her troth, this time joined by Darnell and her publicist. "'Oh Linda,' I wailed, clutching her. "I'm going to be so happy."[26]

Soon discovering she was pregnant, she enjoyed wedded bliss—until discovering her husband was, in fact, still married, his divorce not yet finalized. While working to save her baby—her white blood cell count now dangerously high—she had the marriage annulled. Once the divorce was finalized, though, Stephen begged her to remarry him, and she relented, becoming Mrs. Crane a second time, just as his draft number came up. Their baby girl, Cheryl, was born on July 25, 1943, prematurely, but she survived. The marriage was not so lucky.

Stephen, always bringing his Army buddies home to see his celebrity wife, flunked the physical for a Navy commission, after which he began gambling, arriving home just as Lana was heading out for the studio's early morning call. The final straw came when she visited his hometown in Indiana and discovered his family's "tobacco business" was a tobacconist shop. She divorced him in August 1944, though they maintained their friendship for Cheryl's sake.

On New Year's Day 1945, at age twenty-four, she became the most highly paid actress in the world, earning four thousand dollars a week. She was soon living a fittingly glamorous life in a large house on Belair Country Club's ninth hole, providing her mother a home of her own. While making *The Postman Always Rings Twice* (1946), she started seeing Tyrone Power. They were the talk of the town. But when he wandered off to new pastures, their relationship imploded—but not before she became pregnant. Once again, she was pressured to have an abortion for selfish career considerations—hers and his.

He was the only one to break her heart, she writes, prompting her to flee to New York, where, by day, she was busy with publicity for *Cass Timberlane* (1947) costarring Spencer Tracy; by night, she was squired around town by a new gentleman.

His name was Henry J. "Bob" Topping Jr., heir to the tinplate fortune. During filming, he had flooded her dressing room with roses. Though he had a history of quickie marriages, and was not exactly Cary Grant in the looks department, he wined and dined her and lavished her with presents. Asking her to marry him, he invited her to his family's six-hundred-acre estate, "Round Hill," in Greenwich, Connecticut, with a lake and Tudor-style mansion, where everyone, it seemed, slept with everyone else's wife. Though Topping lacked a moral compass, she had learned to love him. One night he put a fifteen-carat marquise diamond engagement ring in a martini at the '21' Club for her to fish out after which they were married in a traditional Presbyterian wedding ceremony; though, she writes, "the Los Angeles presbytery formally rebuked our minister for performing the ceremony."[27]

During their marriage, lasting 1948–1952, she had two miscarriages, while he returned to his bachelor ways—until finally he dumped her. Devastated, she attempted suicide by a sleeping pill overdose and slitting her wrist just before beginning filming on *The Merry Widow* (1952). Miraculously she was saved—with no one the wiser—and Fernando Llamas helped her recover until Lex Barker, a Princeton grad, who played "Tarzan," cozied up to her one day at a pool party.

The Bad and the Worst

As she continued recovering, she poured herself into *The Bad and the Beautiful*, a tale of Hollywood backstabbing, directed by Vincent Minnelli, eerily featuring a conversation with costar Kirk Douglas, who asks, "How many times have you tried to commit suicide?"

Marrying Barker—her fourth husband—in Turin, Italy, the nuptials lasted 1953–1957, during which she had a third and final miscarriage. His male ego was hurt—she was the bigger star, making films such as *The Sea Chase* (1955) with John Wayne. So he began an affair, a friend informed her, with an actress on a low-budget Universal film.

No sooner had Barker exited, than one nightmare of a year began in April 1957 when a man by the name of John Steele, claiming to be Ava Gardner's friend, began stalking her. Told by an unnamed Hollywood friend that his real name was Johnnie Stompanato, a mafia boss's operative, she felt trapped and tried to deal with the situation herself, feeling oddly attracted to him. Friends begged her to get help.

She began coping by drinking. While not an alcoholic, she writes, she "used vodka to blur the edges, even the center of my life."[28] That and work. She would soon begin filming *Peyton Place* (1957), on her new Universal contract, while he kept turning up wherever in the world she was and taking over.

By April 1958, having just moved into a smaller house in Beverly Hills, she triumphantly attended the Academy Awards as a Best Actress Oscar nominee. When she came home later that night, he was inside, threatening to kill her. Cheryl, overhearing his threats, landed a life-ending thrust with a kitchen knife, an act the court deemed "justifiable homicide."

After "the happening," she writes, "I spent that week under almost continuous sedation, with moments of dark despair."[29] The day her daughter was acquitted, Lana could not stop repeating, "Thank God."[30]

Universal Pictures, gambling on Lana in the aftermath, offered her the lead role in its remake of *Imitation of Life* (1959). In exchange for a minimal fee she accepted half of the profits, a new trend in the fast-changing film business, now that the studio, star-centered system was gone. The gamble paid off and rescued Lana psychologically and financially.

While exhaling, in May 1959, and enjoying a much-needed respite, she met a man at a Malibu party by the name of Fred May. Though an "inner voice" told her "emotional entanglements" brought only sorrow, another part of her craved "a man" for the "warmth, caring and love"[31] he would bring. By 1960, she married this down-to-earth entrepreneur and began a peaceful life with him at his Chino ranch. But the polar opposites began to clash, and by 1962 they were divorced.

With a new lease on life, she finally accepted Bob Hope's invite to join him on a USO tour—this one to the Far East. But by 1964, again longing for love, she met an aspiring actor, ten years her junior, named Bob Eaton, who warned her about a swindler to whom she had lent five thousand dollars. After marrying him in 1965, she made a second USO "handshake" tour, this one to Vietnam in 1967. Upon returning home, she found that he had been unfaithful to her in their bed during one of his nonstop parties. They were divorced in 1969.

Even worse, was the swindler who next wormed his way into her life, promising the moon, only so he could lasso the star and her financial assets. His name was Ronald Dante. They married in 1969. In 1972, he borrowed $35,000 then disappeared. Though most of the money was recovered, he later stole $100,000 worth of her jewelry.

Now, finally chastened, she knew it was time to make a change. "With the exception of dear Fred May," she writes, "all my husbands were takers...I was always a giver, even as a little girl."[32] She proceeded to reinvent herself, once again pouring herself into her work. She had done TV, starring in *The Survivors* (1969), and now turned to theater, starting with *Forty Carats*, making $17,500 a week.

But something was still missing.

A New Woman

By 1980, she was hardly eating and mostly drinking, her weight was down, and she was very ill. Seeing what "a total mess" she was, her friend Eric Root referred her to a holistic specialist, who asked her, "Are you willing to give up alcohol to get your health back?"[33]

"A light came right straight down to my head," she writes, "a light from God, and I said.... 'You've got a deal.'...and, when we shook hands, it was a three-way partnership—God, the doctor and me."[34]

This change was not easy, but, she writes, "When you accept God, you're never alone. With His help, I entered a new phase of my life."[35] And while, she writes, she was never as devout a Catholic as her ex-husband, Stephen, who converted after their divorce,[36] she still found sustenance in the faith.

In 1992—ten years after her autobiography was published— she was diagnosed with throat cancer, which she fought and beat. That May, she contracted a lung infection. "It was not cancer. It was not pneumonia. They didn't know what it was," she told Robin Leach, TV host of *Lifestyles of the Rich and Famous* on November 13, 1994. She later found out, they had given her seven days to live. "But, I walked out of there in seven days—having gained seven pounds," she said.

"That was a manifestation of God's. He himself, I could hear (saying).... 'No, I'm not through with her yet.... I have much more work for her to do *in my name*.' And, every day that I awake, I have joy in my heart and I have peace of mind. And no person, place or thing can take that away from me because God is within me."[37]

This TV interview with Robin Leach would be her last. In her final years, he was the only one she spoke with. She had been silent for ten years. "Fame," said Leach, "drove her ever further from the public gaze."[38]

Clad in a bright purple dress, against which was set a tiny crucifix necklace complemented by two long crystalline strands of beads, she was as feisty, elegant—and 'brave'—as ever during the interview.

The legendary star is shown lighting a candle and praying fervently in the Cathedral of the Good Shepherd in San Sebastian, Spain, in the heart of Basque country. (She had traveled there to receive a lifetime achievement award at the San Sebastian International Film Festival.) Setting the scene, the camera dramatically pulls back from the highest point of the Gothic edifice, a stained glass image of Mary, the Mother of Jesus, streaming light, as if from a celestial perch.

In March 1994, the throat cancer had come back with a vengeance. She was now fighting it "with chemotherapy treatments and with her faith," said Leach.

"Do you pray for relief from the throat cancer?" asked Leach. Her response was classic Lana: "In my particular way: I say, 'Now, look, Power Partner.' That's what I call him. Yeah, I do," she said with a smile. "He is my power partner. And, as I say, He is within me, so I know where all the good stuff is coming from. I say, I don't want this, and I will not have it. So, now will you give me another miracle, please? I'm open, receptive, I'm ready. Let's go for it. How many more shots do I have to take? Just take it away, way, way, way."[39]

"This entire experience did change your life, didn't it?" asked Leach.

"Yes, completely. I'm such a different woman today…I'm strong, I'm healthy, I'm loving, and I'm enthusiastic about life… [and] oh so happy. I just bubble all the time. I hope I don't make a fool of myself. But, to have all this joy inside, it just has to come out."[40]

"The kind of inner peace" she gained from God, she told Leach, is not something she felt during her Hollywood glory days, while embracing all her gorgeous leading men.

Reflecting on her past life and the bad decisions she made, she said, "There's a 'Lana used to be' and there's a 'Lana now.' And the 'Lana used to be' many things she didn't do. The 'Lana now' realizes the 'Lana used to be' was *a fool*. But she was shy and retiring."

Regarding all the men in her life, she said, "I was searching, searching for something and foolishly I turned to someone else. I did not search within myself."

Asked if she was "frightened of death," she said, "No, if God says, 'I've given you enough, now I have other things for you to do,' I'm ready."

She died on June 29, 1995, having found her true love at long last—ready with her new role…in Heaven.

Chapter Eleven

• • •

BETTY HUTTON'S
MIRACULOUS RECOVERY

• • •

I never went on the stage without praying. And, when I got to Hollywood, it started to slowly go out of my system, and I got into trouble.

—BETTY HUTTON TO MIKE DOUGLAS,
The Mike Douglas Show, February 25, 1977

Betty Hutton, glittering star of Hollywood during World War II and the postwar era, sang and acted her way into everyone's heart. Yet, her own heart was troubled, the seeds of which were planted in her fatherless, impoverished childhood. Eleven years after she rocketed to the top, her star fell precipitously. In his waning days, Paramount's A.C. Lyles reminisced to me about his friend, Betty, confiding how "badly" he felt about the ordeal she had suffered.[1] Miraculously, God used her suffering to transform her heart and bring her healing.

"What Price Genius?"
Betty Hutton was all heart—and totally vulnerable. It was the secred of her success—and her suffering. Constance Collier, as Miss Gibbs in *The Perils of Pauline*, summed it up perfectly when she said to Hutton, playing Pearl White:

139

Child, never forget this moment—this happiness—not even if they've broken your heart and you're trying to put the pieces back together again...you've a brave heart, child. And brave hearts, like all rare and fine things, are easily broken.

This vulnerability—and strength—came through in a conversation she had in 1936 with Al Jolson, star of the first "talkie," *The Jazz Singer* (1927). Just fifteen, she had escaped to New York for a visit: "'Mr. Jolson, I am so scared.' And, he said, 'Good, kid. I throw up before each show.' He said, 'Betty, if you lose that, you're through.'"[2]

Betty got her first break closer to home when bandleader Vincent Lopez scouted her. It was January 16, 1938. She was performing with a local Detroit band, and he hired her on the spot as his lead vocalist, changing her name to Hutton. To celebrate, she ate steak for the first time in her life—at breakfast, lunch, dinner, and supper!

But while touring around the country with "Vince Lopez and his Orchestra," seventeen-year-old Betty began worrying she wasn't connecting with her audience. In Philadelphia a trombonist confirmed this, warning her she was about to get fired. With that, Betty gulped down three Brandy & Benedictines and arrived at the theater feeling she had "nothing to lose. I sat on the musicians' laps, pulled their hair and threw myself around a lot. The audience loved me."[3]

Their love filled a deep void.

Hardscrabble Early Life

Born Betty June Thornburg in Battle Creek, Michigan, on February 26, 1921, Hutton never knew her father, Percy "Jack" Thornburg. A railroad brakeman, born in Nebraska in 1896, he skipped town with another woman when Betty was two.

Her mother was also born Nebraska, in 1901, and lost her own mother to pneumonia when she was nine, after which her father regularly beat her up. Moral and hardworking, she escaped to Battle Creek, Michigan, where she lived with an aunt and railroad executive uncle, who arranged for her to marry Jack when she was sixteen. The couple settled in Calhoun, Michigan, where they were living at the time of the 1920 census with their daughter, Marion. In 1923, Mabel moved Betty and Marion to Lansing to start a new life and Jack began anew in Los Angeles.

Once in Lansing, Mabel opened a Prohibition-era "Blind Pig," providing "beer and bathtub gin" to thirsty customers and ready cash for her family. With "no education," she would do almost anything to keep from accepting welfare with social workers calling the shots.[4] "I started singing at three

Betty Hutton with her mother, Mabel, and older sister, Marion

years old on top of the kitchen table—singing 'Black Bottom, she's got 'em,'" she told Mike Douglas, and she sang the song for him, thumping her thigh.[5] Her earliest memory, she told TCM host Robert Osbourne—"like it was yesterday"—dated back to the same timeframe, in 1924, when she spontaneously broke into song to distract a drunken man threatening to beat up her mother. Gradually, Betty was joined by her older sister, Marion, and they became regular entertainers at the speakeasy, a constantly changing venue, two steps ahead of the police.

"I had lived on poverty row," she said later. "My goal was to save my mother.... I wanted my mother to be a lady. All my life I had seen her falling down drunk. Men would spit on her and say: 'Look at the drunken broad.'"[6]

In the midst of this moral filth, a rose of faith would grow. As she told Douglas:

> When I was a little girl, I didn't know about God. My mother was an atheist. And, the nuns were right across the street from us. And, sometimes I had to run from the brutal stuff going on. And, they would hide me in their skirts. I wasn't a Catholic and [non-Catholics] weren't allowed to go to Catholic school. But, they would take me and they taught me Catechism…and I learned about God.[7]

In 1929 the family moved to Detroit, where her take-charge mother soon landed an auto factory job. It was in upholstery, paying twenty-two cents an hour, her mouth all marked at day's end from holding nails and tacks between her lips as she worked to affix fabric to the seats. While there, she organized her factory union. Still, life was hard and Mabel was hard drinking—forcing eight-year-old Betty to sing on street corners for small change.

Her mother discovered Betty had real talent at age nine when she sang in a school production, after which she began taking Betty around Detroit to perform for any group that would listen. Later, when her mother took her to see a Charlie Chaplin silent film, Betty thought, "I'm gonna be a star and my mother will stop drinking."[8] ("She got sober when I was 20," Betty told Douglas, "but that took a lot of praying.")[9]

After resuming her schooling, she finally quit for good in the ninth grade, at age thirteen, to earn money ironing shirts and doing housework, while continuing to sing. "I had a great desire to lift myself up, out of the mess. I believed a power, God, would help me. So I prayed simply. I just said, 'God, please help me. I've got to make it.'…I always knew I could be a star."[10]

Finding Love from Audiences

Her chat with Al Jolson paid off. She got that local gig—but not before receiving shocking news via telegram from her father. It was his suicide note dated August 26, 1937, the day he died. He wired one hundred dollars to each of his two daughters.[11] They had not heard from him since 1923. A veteran, he was buried at Los Angeles National Cemetery.

Bereft of fatherly love, Betty was getting "love" from audiences. "Applause was my love, or rather a substitute for love."[12]

By 1939, she was back in New York at Billy Rose's Casa Manana[13] with Lopez, Rose warning her not to "tear up the place."[14] She dazzled audiences—including Buddy DeSylva, who, coincidentally, cowrote the hit song for the "Black Bottom" dance. (Released on June 28, 1926, it soon eclipsed the "Charleston.")

Launching out on her own, she made her Broadway debut in *Two for the Road* on February 8, 1940, and by August, was tapped for Cole Porter's *Panama Hattie* starring Ethel Merman. But Merman cut Betty's only solo number and Betty was crestfallen. DeSylva, who was producing, said, "Hold it, that's her contract,"[15] while confiding to Betty he was slated to head Paramount production, promising to make her a star—if she would stick with the show. That she did until June 1, 1941.

A Star Is Born

"I remember Betty the first day she came to Paramount," A.C. said, and how she "brought the house down" at a show at Shriner Auditorium that same week. She was quickly cast in *The Fleet's In* (1942), starring William Holden, and "just exploded on the screen," said A.C, with her trademark exuberant performance of "Arthur Murray Taught Me Dancing in a Hurry." "A vitamin pill with legs," quipped Bob Hope, on whose radio show she negotiated a thirteen-week run shortly after the film's debut.[16]

"From there," said A.C., "she just became one of the most important stars we've ever had at Paramount, and made picture after picture after picture"—fourteen in the 1940s (nineteen in all). Along the way, she became a hit recording artist with such chart toppers as Hoagy Carmichael's "Doctor, Lawyer, Indian Chief" (*The Stork Club*) and a popular live performer. She also managed to get married in 1945 to camera manufacturer Ted Briskin, with whom she had two children, Lindsay Diane Briskin (b. 1946) and Candice Elizabeth Briskin (b. 1947) But he wanted her to stay home, and by 1950, they were divorced, reuniting for a time.

Then, at twenty-nine, she got the role of a lifetime—Annie Oakley in MGM's *Annie Get Your Gun* (1950), based on George Gershwin's Broadway musical—replacing an exhausted Judy Garland. It was also, she told TCM's Robert Osbourne, "the heartbreak" of her life. MGM did not even invite her to the premiere in New York on May 17.

Up next: Cecil B. DeMille's *The Greatest Show on Earth*, about the Ringling Brothers Barnum and Bailey Circus. Gambling she would get the lead role, she learned to fly through the air from a world-renowned aerialist. When it came time to perform for DeMille, "She sent a big wreath of flowers," said A.C. and "said, come to Stage 5, I have surprise." DeMille, "was just not only amazed but intrigued" at her performance, and she got the lead, said A.C., receiving "top billing above Charleton Heston and so many big, big stars." The picture won DeMille the Oscar.

Personal and Professional Unraveling

In December 1950, poised to begin filming in Sarasota, Florida, she split once and for all from Briskin, citing "mental cruelty." When the divorce was finalized in January 1951, she writes, "I took my first pill," Dexamil,[17] to deal with multiple stresses, including marital difficulties and a challenging film, which required a starvation diet because, she writes, "the skimpy circus costumes revealed everything."[18]

She was just getting started. Dexamil, "an amphetamine, later known as street speed," used to increase energy while curbing one's appetite, "was given out freely," she writes. Unaware of the crippling side effects, she rushed to the doctor for this "simple pep-me-up" that would also "control my weight" and increase self-esteem, making her, she writes, "more sociable and quite self-confident." She was also prescribed Dexadrine, given to Air Force pilots on long missions so they could stay alert. If it was good enough for America's heroes, it was good enough for her, she thought. Then, to counteract the effects of sleeplessness, she began increasing her doses of sleeping pills. "I had no clue," she writes, "but the pills were to become a major vice, and led to my eventual and complete downfall."

As she finished production on *The Greatest Show on Earth* in July 1951, her voice was about to give out. But there was no rest for the weary. On August 26, she began filming *Somebody Loves Me* (1952), her third biopic—having previously played Texas Guinan and Pearl White—this one about vaudeville singer Blossom Seeley.

As 1952 dawned, her career was winding down; the scripts were poor, she said. The final straw was Paramount's refusal to let her new husband, choreographer Charles O'Curran, direct her next film. She had married him on March 8, 1952, two months after *The Greatest Show on Earth* premiered. Unwisely, she was trying to boost his career. In the process she was torpedoing her own.

"When they said no," A.C. said at her memorial service, "she told them to rip up her contract and they obliged."[19] It was July 18, 1952. The same day, Hutton announced plans to produce films on a partnership basis with her husband. O'Curran was no Paramount.

"That was the biggest mistake Betty ever made. Paramount never opened the doors to her again. Then the demons took over. Betty wasn't a difficult lady—she was impossible," A.C. said.[20]

Asked about the notion that the scripts were inferior, he said, it's important to understand that "Betty had somewhat of a persecution complex. And, she was a lady who had torments; but tremendous, tremendous talents... And, they all showed up on the screen."

On September 29, 1952, having turned her back on Hollywood, Betty opened at the London Palladium, for four weeks. The following July, she began "playing in Vegas" and her drug habit, which had begun in Florida in 1951, "got out of range," said Carl Bruno, executor of her estate.

As Betty told it, "The old snap wasn't there, the shows were too hard. My mother gave me a little tiny Dexamil [a stimulant].... It was innocent as that, and I said 'That's it! I'm not tired!'... It led to a vicious cycle, pills to get 'up,' pills to calm down."[21]

Judy Garland and Betty, sharing the same demons, became close in Vegas, where Betty was earning $150,000 weekly—$100,000 a show when she filled in for Judy.[22] She even broke Judy's attendance record when she opened at the Palace Theatre on Broadway on October 14, 1953.[23] Her nightclub act at the Desert Inn, Edith

Gwynn reported, got rare Vegas "raves." Three days later, on July 20, 1953, Betty collapsed before her show, telling the press she "got too much sunshine."[24] Make that sunshine in a pill.

In May 1954, NBC announced she had been chosen for *Satins and Spurs*, a musical Broadway spectacular tailored for television. Stresssing over her appearance, she fired O'Curran, who was initially directing, and they were divorced by July 1. Hyped as one of TV's first broadcasts in color—at a time when color TV sets were rare—predictably, when the millions gathered around their black-and-white sets in living rooms and did not see color, ratings tanked.

That November she gave what was billed as her final cabaret performance in Las Vegas. "It was a terribly emotional night," she recalled. "Women cried and men stormed the stage shouting, 'No! No!'"[25] But her retirement was short-lived. Her attempt two years later at a Hollywood comeback, in a minor film—her final—titled *Spring Reunion* (1957), was a flop and garnered few notices.

Scrambling to recover the shambles of her career, in 1959, she invested $600,000 of her own money in a TV show called "The Betty Hutton Show," a Desilu sitcom featuring "Goldie" (Hutton) announced on March 20—after which she filed for divorce from Alan Livingston, a recording company executive, whom she had married in 1955. The show did not fare any better than the rocky marriage and was canceled within months.

On Christmas Eve 1960, at age thirty-nine after barely catching her breath, she was back at the altar, marrying jazz trumpeter Pete Candoli, two years her junior. Having returned to her religious roots, they wed at the Lutheran Church of the Reformation in Las Vegas and planned a six-month honeymoon in Europe. But, in April 1961, in London, Betty announced she was getting an annulment.

Then, on New Year's Eve, her mother died in a fire. Pregnant with her third child, she was advised not to attend the funeral, lest the stress impact her pregnancy. Her daughter, Carolyn "Cary" Candoli was born shortly thereafter.

A few years later, in 1965, at age forty-five, she starred briefly in *Fade In Fade Out* on Broadway, replacing Carol Burnett. But her star had faded.

After signing with Paramount to star in *Red Tomahawk* (1967), a low-budget Western Lyles was producing, featuring *Annie Get Your Gun* costar, Howard Keel, she was replaced shortly after filming began.

Hitting Rock Bottom

Hutton's 1966 was about to get worse. That summer, to her shock, she heard Rona Barrett announce on television that her husband, Pete, was engaged to Edie Adams. The couple separated by August, and divorced twice, first in Juarez, Mexico, in September. "That's the thing that cracked me," she said. "I took a whole bottle of pills and said the hell with it."[26] When she was down, said Michael Mayer, cowriter of *Backstage You Can Have*, that's how she reacted. On November 14, police were called to Betty's South Laguna Beach home for a domestic disturbance, and two days later she was rushed to South Coast Community Hospital after overdosing on sleeping pills.

On March 23, 1967, Betty filed for a U.S. divorce, and on June 18, her divorce was finalized, after which she declared bankruptcy with $150,000 in debts, having fallen from a peak of $10 million in assets.

By 1968, Betty was confined to her bed. Meanwhile, her remaining possessions—the big pieces of furniture—were stolen and sold by a shyster she was living with, who also claimed to be her agent, signing deals on her behalf.

She began living in seedy hotels, or homeless on the street when she could not afford even the minimum of shelter.

Around 1970, as Betty was being thrown out of the latest Hollywood hovel she called home, she was introduced to a minister named Eugene and his partner, Carl Bruno, at a nearby church, who took her in.

"All she had was a shopping bag with a few things in it," said Bruno. "I'll never forget it. She was in one of those leather coats that the women wore in the seventies with the fur collars. And, it was all crinkled and peeling. I mean it was really very sad. And I had no idea who she was." Worth millions a few short years before, she had lost all her money—and her singing voice.

Six months later, her daughter, Cary, joined her mother at her new home in the Hollywood Hills, and over the next year or so, Betty regained a measure of her strength. Yet, by 1971, Betty Hutton—age fifty, surveying four shattered marriages and a wrecked career—was on track for the same fate as Judy Garland, whose life ended two years before of a drug overdose. "I wanted to die," she said.[27]

In 1972, she was on the road performing shortly after losing custody of her youngest daughter. "I tried to commit suicide," she said. "It was the end of the road for me."[28] "I was on so many uppers and downers there weren't enough pills to put me up or bring me down," she said.[29] She was checked into a rehab hospital outside Boston, named Greyrock, and treated for depression. "I weighed only 85 pounds and looked more dead than alive."[30]

Then, something miraculous happened.

"God Touched Me"

On the verge of giving up—"stone sober, dressed in a showbiz white pantsuit," plotting her next move—she looked out the window and saw this priest calmly helping an out-of-control drunk woman. "He never lost his gentleness. The language coming out of the woman was disgusting. She started vomiting on" him. At that moment, she said, "God touched me."[31] And she thought, "I'm going to meet that man. He's going to save my life."

The priest's name was Fr. Peter McGuire. He was the pastor at St. Anthony's Church in Portsmouth, Rhode Island, and was also a counselor. He had come to Boston to check his cook into the same rehab facility.

"He was a wonderful man," said Professor James Hersh, Salve Regina University's Philosophy Chair, who knew Hutton well. "I can see why she was so drawn to him."[32]

Fr. Maguire initially had no idea he had made any particular impression on Betty. He didn't even know who she was. But the minute his cook was well enough to converse, Betty asked about him and learned he was a saint who helped everyone.

"When you sat down with that man, and you talked to him," said Bruno, "it was like talking to God...there was just an aura about him." His appearance, said Bruno, didn't matter to him. "He had holes in his shoes and...an old wrinkled up suit on." Betty, who dressed flawlessly, he said, would, in time, suggest sartorial improvements.

But now, she needed help—on the inside. So she asked the cook, "what if you get drunk and can't cook." "Want to go with me?"[33] she asked. Hutton soon decamped to Newport—as far from the Hollywood limelight as anyplace. As she said on *Good Morning America* in August 1978:

If I hadn't gotten (to Newport), I wouldn't have made it. They didn't expect me to be super great here. These people... took me in their homes, their little homes, and held me in their arms and kissed me and hugged me back to life. And, that's New England, boy.

"Thank God," said Lyles, "for Fr. Maguire because he probably saved her life.... And, that was a period of hardship and work for her."

"I lived on the third floor of the rectory," she told the *Boston Globe*. "It was an attic. A dark attic," prompting her to sometimes think, "What the hell am I doing here?"[34] She didn't stay long. In the summer of 1973, feeling like a fish out of water, she joined a summer stock group, performing Cole Porter's *Anything Goes* in Connecticut, Massachusetts, and Rhode Island. One night at the Chateau de Ville Dinner Theatre in Framingham, she went into a meltdown. An anonymous blogger describes the evening:

Once on stage, she took some bows and suddenly started to cry.... After a few minutes the applause died down, the house went silent, and we sat...expecting the show to start. Betty then...uttered the words "Remember this one?"... and broke into the song "Friendship."... She then started to talk about her marriage to Pete.... After what seemed like a very long time, the show finally started.... Betty was not in good voice...and she wept through most of the songs.... It sounded disastrous [but the audience clapped].... Still microphoned and weeping at the end of the number we heard her exclaim "Oh my God, they still love me!"[35]

By early fall, she was back at the rectory—cooking, washing dishes, making beds, cleaning—enduring her lowly role by pretending she was playing Bernadette Soubirous (Jennifer Jones) in *The Song of Bernadette* (1943). Furthermore, she said, "Father

Betty Hutton pouring coffee for Fr. Peter Maguire (right) and Fr. James Hamilton (left)

Maguire was not someone I had to impress. He certainly didn't expect me to sleep with him and he didn't care that I had been a star. He just took the time to talk with me. It took a long time to get the pain out."[36]

In 1974, news of her newfound life hit the papers, after which her delicate recovery began to unravel. At her lowest ebb, Earl Wilson, entertainment columnist for *The New York Post*, organized a "Love In" benefit for her in New York. "I haven't got a cent," Betty told the assembled guests. Later in the year she entered a mental hospital for treatment.[37]

During her five-year long recovery, as she struggled to regain her strength and overcome her addictions, she also lived in Newport and other nearby locations, to be near Father Maguire.

"You're Just a Very Hurt Child"

"I never found me until Fr. Maguire," she told Osbourne. "I [was] the product," she said, "like hamburgers, hotdogs." "Fr. Maguire had the heart to understand me… [and] he knew all the background of the alcohol." For the first time in her life, she said, she didn't have to pretend she wasn't upset.

"'Betty, you're just a very hurt child. Let's start from the word go,' she told Osbourne he said to her. "He loved me, Bob." He had "Christ's love—it totally surrounds you…[and was] like…the wonderful men… Jesus said in the Bible he was going to leave."

He would talk with her, at times, for seven hour stretches and began tutoring her to bridge her educational gap. He also taught her about the Catholic faith, after which she decided to convert.

"When I became a Catholic," she told Osbourne, "it was so great because as I walked down the aisle and I know I'm going to receive Christ, I would sob so because this brought something out of me I never knew was in there. That's my heart. *Christ* is my heart. But, I didn't know him. I *did not know* God."

Hutton also cultivated a special devotion to Our Lady. "I don't move anywhere without my rosary" she said, "because I know I'm scared inside. I'm always scared. I'm never secure."[38]

New Roles

Fr. Maguire taught her the subjects she had missed from the ninth grade to the twelfth grade, an amazing feat he gradually accomplished over ten years.[39]

Meanwhile, she began performing for Catholic groups and worked alongside Fr. Maguire with down-and-out people, which, she told Osbourne, was her "niche." "If I can take a soul that nobody wants any part of and pull them up by their bootstraps; that is a joy." She would also generously share her culinary creations when she learned of a particular need. And starting in 1978, she began speaking about addiction problems, initially in New England before small groups, then around the country. She also worked as a publicist in the late seventies for a jai alai palace in Newport.

In September 1980, she returned to Broadway for the musical *Annie*, playing Miss Hannigan for two weeks. Her grandchildren came to see her, which was "one of the great thrills of her life."[40]

Two years later, she performed at Capitol Records' Fortieth Anniversary tribute and was the "emotional highlight."[41] The following March, she starred in PBS's *Juke Box Saturday Night*, clutching the rosary Father Maguire had given throughout.

"God's plan," she told the *New York Times*, would determine her showbiz future.

God had other plans.

Fr. McGuire, she told Osbourne, had "put all these books in my hands and when I felt I was ready I said, Father, I want to go to college." In September 1983, at age sixty-two, Hutton enrolled as a student at Salve Regina University. Just like in her films, Hersh said, Hutton had "huge childlike energy" and "loved learning… and threw herself into it."

"Being" Betty in Newport

In the early eighties, Hutton had settled into a mansion overlooking Newport Harbor and, for once in her life, enjoyed just being Betty. She called her bedroom, "a womb with a view," her close friend, who prefers to remain anonymous, said. "Betty loved the coming and going, the yachts, conjuring up images of her Hollywood days, the Canadian geese, the serenity of the water, and Newport Bridge in the distance because it was designed by a woman!" said her friend.

"Her private life," Hersh explained, "had been the source of so much pain that she was sort of setting it right. And, Newport was the place to undergo that transformation and]… recapture who she was not on stage."

As Hersh tells it, one day in his Philosophy of Imagination course, they were discussing what Swiss psychologist Carl Jung calls "the shadow," where "right under the surface of the unconscious is an archetypal figure that everybody has that represents what he called our 'inferior character traits'—everything that we work as individuals to overcome."

"Boy," said Hersh, "that hit home with Betty."

For her class presentation, she disappeared and came back in tights with top hat and cane and "did a little soft shoe" while singing "Me and My Shadow" a cappella. "It was so tender," he said, "because she was singing with tears just streaming down her cheeks." The students, he said, were bewildered. "But, I knew who she was and I knew what she had been through and seen her films and then to see her in this situation was an extraordinary experience."

Betty receiving an honorary degree in 1984

Hutton described for him the "wall between her show biz experience [where she found happiness *on stage*] and the real world." It was obvious, he said, "she was looking for a father."

"People loved her," said Hersh. "They really appreciated what she was as herself."

And she stayed in touch with her Hollywood friends, including A.C., whom she would call every now and again, telling him how happy she was and asking about everyone.

In September 1984, she was awarded an honorary doctorate. Twenty months later, she graduated cum laude from Salve Regina with a master's degree in Liberal Studies.

She graduated on May 18, 1986. "Grasping the diploma with both hands," *The Providence Journal* reported, "she kept her left hand clenched around a strand of green ceramic rosary beads. Before descending to take her seat, she lifted the diploma heavenward and raised her eyes in a silent gesture of thanks."[42] (The beads were the ones Fr. Maguire had given her.)

After graduating, Betty taught drama at Salve Regina, which she told Osbourne, "was a neat job because then I could begin to give Betty to them—not just the commodity, the hotdog." That included counseling "kids on drugs." She also taught comedy and oral interpretation at Boston's Emerson College for a semester.

Her close friend said how spiritual she was, "There wasn't a minute when she wasn't praying. She had an aura about her and could almost divine what was in souls."

"Practically all the stars are in trouble," Hutton told priests she met in Rhode Island. "You happen to see me talking honestly to you. It's a nightmare out there! It hurts what we do in our private lives."[43]

She shared Fr. Maguire's fervor for souls, who, after retiring, worked with ill veterans, telling her when one had gone to confession, "I roped another one, Betty."[44]

The Father She Never Had

She always said of Fr. Maguire, "He was my father." And Fr. Maguire, like a good father, always said of Betty—"What price genius?"[45]

On July 8, 1996, he died after years of battling diabetes and heart disease. Losing Fr. Maguire "was just so painful to me," she told Osbourne, "I couldn't handle it."

In March 1997, she moved to Palm Springs to be closer to her family. Ten years later, on March 11, 2007, suffering from complications of colon cancer, she received the last rites, slipping away just before midnight—into the arms of her Heavenly Father.

Chapter Twelve
• • •

ANN MILLER'S QUEST FOR
SPIRITUAL GOLD

• • •

I think it was a very daring thing my mother did, bringing me to Hollywood and putting me to work in that 'jungle out there,' as she called it, at such a young age. But I survived the jungle with a sense of ideals, which is the best thing that can happen to you in this town. If you come out of it with ideals, you have a handful of gold.[1]

—ANN MILLER

Ann Miller—dynamic dancing, singing, and acting talent, known for *You Can't Take It With You* (1938), *Easter Parade* (1948), and *Kiss Me Kate* (1953)—rose to the status of a leading lady only later in life, when she costarred on Broadway with Mickey Rooney in *Sugar Babies* (1979–1982).

She did it the right way, by dint of hard work—a slower but truer rise. "I never played politics, I was never a party girl, and I never slept with any of the producers," she said.[2] She also had all the requisite imperfections. "We have our own wars within our souls, and special ways of killing our mental dragons," she writes. "I'm a clothesaholic."[3] And she saved everything—probably, she writes, for fear of returning to her poor antecedents. In the end she also saved her soul.

Poor Beginnings—"Annie's" Talent Providing Hope
She was born "Johnnie" Lucille Collier on April 12, 1923, at St. Joseph's Hospital in Houston, Texas, to a nearly deaf mother of Cherokee descent named Clara Emma Birdwell. Her father, John Alfred Collier, of Irish and French descent, rose from poverty, supporting himself through law school as a barber. He became a criminal lawyer, representing Bonnie and Clyde, Baby Face Nelson, and Machine Gun Kelly. At heart, writes Ann, he was "an Irish playboy," who became intoxicated with his success. He named his daughter Johnnie because he wanted a boy. The name Lucille was for her maternal great grandmother, a psychic, whom, she writes, "predicted I would have the 'gift.'"[4]

At age five, Annie, as her mother called her, developed rickets. So Clara enrolled her in ballet lessons to strengthen her legs. "Or at least that was the excuse," Ann writes. "That and the gypsy fortune teller" they encountered while waiting at a Houston bus stop in the boiling humidity en route to visit her grandparents in Chireno. This scruffy seer sidled up to them and, after Clara greased her palm with a silver half-dollar, predicted, "She will be a star for many years. I see music and lights and dancing and money. Take her to the West—when you marriage ends—for there she will become a Child of Destiny." Afterward Clara constantly nagged Annie to "rehearse, REHEARSE, REHEARSE," sometimes to the point she wanted to pop.[5]

That same year, she had her first psychic experience—envisioning her father with a dark haired woman in a boat in the park. Later that day, when he was tardy, claiming work had detained him, she quizzed him about his boating excursion with this woman, and he got very angry, prompting him finally to ask how she knew that, pressing her until she said, "I just know it. I saw it...I don't know how."[6]

Meanwhile her mother signed Annie up for violin lessons. One day she smashed the violin over her teacher's head, exasperated at how she would chomp on fudge during the 4 P.M. lessons, without sharing any while Annie's stomach growled from hunger. She didn't fare any better with piano lessons. "And, ballet," she writes, was "almost as bad. I felt like a big crow flapping with those long legs and arms."

"It was the great Negro tap dancer Bill Robinson, Mr. 'Bojangles' himself," she writes "who gave me my first tap lesson and changed the course of my life." After his show at the Majestic Theatre in Houston, her mother took her backstage, and she performed a dance for him. "I'll never forget how nice and kind and patient Bill Robinson was with us. He watched my little ballet number. Then he did a few taps for me and asked me to try to tap along with him. He sang 'Bye, Bye, Blues' and clapped out the rhythm with his hands, and there I was doing my first tap dance with Mr. 'Bojangles' in his dressing room."[7] After that, she writes, she knew her mother was right. She would become a dancer. She began practicing incessantly and was a smash hit at the Big Brothers Club in Houston, sporting a fancy Egyptian costume her parents bought.

Both Clara and John were convinced of their daughter's talent but agreed on little else. The tension in their marriage caused Annie to become "withdrawn and lonely." Rather than returning home after school to witness their fights, she preferred escaping to a wooded area behind Sutton Elementary School she called "the enchanted forest." There she'd carry on conversations with the deer, frogs, and squirrels. At the same time, the reason Clara constantly nagged her to practice became clear. "Someday," she said, "you may have to take care of your mother."[8]

Something died inside of her when she realized what it meant when her father went off with other women. Then, one day, when he was teaching her how to swim in Galveston, he promised he'd be there for her. Instead, he jerked her away and ordered her to swim, and she almost drowned. After that, she lost all trust in her father.

His marital infidelity reached a tipping point when Clara and Annie returned early from visiting the grandparents one day and found John in a vividly compromising position with another woman, prompting Annie to tell her mother, "I will take care of you, Mother. You don't need my father." They immediately headed west—for good—driving there with John's paramour and her child.[9]

It was 1934.

Once in Hollywood, Annie developed as a dancer, while Clara became the classic 'protective stage mother,' her Baptist strictures ratcheting up the discipline. She had already taken dance lessons in Hollywood that summer and had also gotten calls from Central Casting to be an extra in *Anne of Green Gables* (1934), her first film experience.

They lived in a small one-room kitchenette apartment and had a memorable Christmas marked as it was by the landlady's gift of a chocolate cake. Later, Annie went out to the trash behind the apartment. Rummaging through the magazines and newspapers, she discovered a book opened to a page with this passage underlined: "Have no fear. Have faith. Because I am with you always. If you have the faith of a mustard seed, you can move mountains."[10]

Moving Mountains in Hollywood
Annie soon began studying diligently at nearby Morgan's Dance Shop on Sunset Boulevard after school—across from her former

dance school. The proprietor, Mr. William Morgan, gave Annie her first pair of tap shoes and taught her exercises on a tap board that she practiced faithfully, learning to dance her famous five hundred taps a minute. Soon she was performing at service clubs and began entering amateur contests, which led to a two-week gig with the Keith vaudeville circuit, followed by a regular gig at the Casanova Club on Sunset Boulevard as "Anne Miller." Of course, it was illegal for a minor to be working, but nobody asked any questions. With her long legs and height, now 5'5"—rising to 5'7"—and her bangs grown out by age twelve, making her look older, it seemed natural for her to say she was eighteen.

Her first big booking was at Bal Tabarin nightclub in San Francisco, where, one night Lucille Ball was dazzled by her performance, telling fellow comedian Benny Rubin, "That girl is a marvelous dancer.... She could give Eleanor Powell a run for her money."[11] After making a screen test, she was given a seven-year contract with RKO at $150 a week—her first steady income—and was given a specialty taps number in her first picture, *New Faces of 1937*. Her father, coming through for the first time, provided her with a fake birth certificate, stating that she was born in 1919 not 1923, enabling her to work, now as Ann Miller, age seventeen.

She began to rise fast. In 1938, attending her first Academy Awards, she was seated between Oscar winners, Walt Disney and Hermes Pan. The following year, after making Frank Capra's *You Can't Take It With You* on loan to Columbia, she attended the Academy Awards again, joining Capra, who won the Best Director Oscar.

Now a serious threat to Eleanor Powell, and represented by the same agency, William Morris, her agent arranged for her to play in *George White's Scandals of 1939* on Broadway. If the show was a bomb, they would neatly dispose of Ann Miller. Instead, when it opened at the Alvin Theatre on August 28, 1939, she was the toast of the town, and Hollywood wooed her back. While making *Too Many Girls* (1940) with RKO, she introduced Lucy to Desi Arnaz, then made two pictures for Republic, followed by a little musical for Columbia, leading to a seven-year contract.

Soon thereafter, she bought her first home, a Frank Lloyd Wright in the Hollywood Hills, for her mother and herself and began frequenting Ciro's, Mocambo, and other hot spots where the stars socialized. She was getting noticed. In 1944, she met Louis B. Mayer, head of MGM, through her agent Frank Orsatti. Known as "the Czar of Hollywood," not everyone was enamored of Mayer. But Ann was ever-loyal, writing, "I knew him only as a very kind man with a soft heart, a man who loved beauty and goodness, a man who respected respectability."[12]

And she was respectable. "I became a Hollywood star on my talent, not on casting couches," she writes. "If I had gone that route, I could have been a bigger star. That's the name of the game in Filmlandia."[13] L.B. Mayer, thirty-nine years Ann's senior, was no stranger to women offering sexual favors in exchange for a part. But Ann he respected and wanted to make her his wife. Not realizing how fond Mayer was of her, the twenty-one-year-old began dating a wealthy oilman and steel heir, Reese Milner, whom she met through friends at the Mocambo. When she informed Mayer she was planning to marry him, he was crestfallen and nearly killed himself with an overdose of sleeping pills.

She "blew it,"[14] she thought, in choosing Milner over Mayer. Whether or not Mayer would have made a good husband, one thing's certain, Milner was a tragic choice. She was a virgin at the time of her nuptials, which is rare in Hollywood. The marriage—"a nightmare," she writes, given Milner's Jekyll and Hyde personality—lasted just one year, February 16, 1946, to January 22, 1947. [15]

Harry Cohn tried to warn her. Likewise, her hysterical agents forbade her to marry him. Love is blind, and Ann didn't listen. She married the Texas charmer and soon became pregnant. On November 12, 1946, when she was eight months pregnant, he kicked her down the stairs in a drunken rage, causing her to go into premature labor. That night, she gave birth to a baby girl, Mary Milner, who is buried, alongside her mother, at Holy Cross Cemetery in Culver City, California.

While still healing from broken ribs sustained in the fall, she landed a starring role in *Easter Parade* (1948) after Cyd Charisse bowed out. It was a painful but rewarding experience—Darvon pills getting her through the dance numbers, while her rib cage was taped up. Signing with MGM, Ann soon made several more musicals including *On the Town* (1949) and *Kiss Me Kate* (1953). But the musical was going out of vogue, so she began doing TV, starting in 1953 with the Lux Video Theatre—an adaptation of motion pictures—and continued looking for love, mostly in all the wrong places.

Learning nothing from her first fatally flawed husband, twelve years later she married another loser—by default.

Her true love was an attorney named William V. O'Connor, a devout Catholic, to whom Margaret Pereira, wife of the famous architect, William Pereira, introduced her soon after her divorce from Milner. For twelve years, she hoped against hope that O'Connor's wife, who had left him, would sign the annulment papers. She even began studying to become a Catholic, during which time she was given a tour of the Holy Land—but not before being fingered as an Israeli spy. After convincing officials, she was there because of her interest in Catholicism, the Archdiocese arranged for a personal tour. "Walking where Christ had walked," she writes, "was an awesome, spine-tingling experience,"[16] that only made her more desirous of marrying Bill O'Connor. But Mrs. O'Connor was immovable, and bowing to reality, Ann instead married Bill Moss in 1958. Her close friend Jane Withers, Shirley Temple's costar in *Bright Eyes* (1934) and longtime FOX star, had introduced her to him. We cared about each other," said Withers. "She always had a delightful sense of humor. She was always fun to be with—a magnificent dancer...and she would fall down with laughter," Jane said, when she would impersonate Ann, as she did all the stars of the late 20s and 30s. "And she always liked Bill so much," said Withers, whom she married in 1947, had three children with and later divorced. When Bill began dating Ann, filling the void in her life, Jane warned her that his alcohol and gambling helped destroy their marriage and that "he would get... very unkind when he was drinking." But she didn't listen this time either. The marriage lasted just three years.

During her marriage to Moss, she had a premonition that O'Connor was going to die and insisted to Bill that they return to L.A. Sure enough, he died a few days later.

Still looking for love, in 1961 she married a third and final time, this time to a man, whom, she writes, "thought he was a Beverly Hills Maharajah" and had a lifestyle to match. He also had five ex-wives and sixteen mistresses. They were divorced within a year and obtained an annulment.

Her husbands, she writes, had much in common. All made their fortunes in oil—her Texas roots, she believed, subconsciously attracting her to them. Numbers one and three were

"Texas oil men," while number two hailed "from an old pioneer California family." All three, she writes, "were handsome, rich, utterly charming when...sober." Problem was, at their core, she writes, they were spoiled playboys. "All my husbands wanted to be married bachelors, and I was too dumb to catch on."[17]

Meanwhile her desire to become a Catholic continued to burn brightly. "Only material things are laid at the feet of the Altar of Fame that the great [g]od of Hollywood demands of you," she writes. "And material things cost money."[18] She earned and spent money—lots of it. Becoming a star and staying on top required it. But, in the end, spiritual gold meant the most to her.

Heaven Bound

Father Padraic Loftus, former pastor of St. Mel's in Woodland Hills, California, entered Ann's life at a grace-filled moment, in the waning days of her earthly sojourn, through their mutual friend, June Haver.[19] Fr. Loftus had met June through her sister, Evelyn,[20] who worked for him. Both sisters were Catholic converts.

In November 2003, as usual, June invited him to attend her annual Thanksgiving dinner. This year, however, it was held at the Belair Country Club on Sunset Boulevard. Her husband, Fred MacMurray, had died twelve years earlier, and now, Haver, herself ailing, was unable to host a big dinner party at her home as she had always done.

"So, we were all sitting inside the club," said Fr. Loftus in his lilting Irish accent, and "this lady came in. She was a bit late." It was Ann Miller. As June's daughter, Katie, went over to greet her, said Fr. Loftus, "Ann looked over at his table and asked her, 'Who is that priest sitting over there beside your mother?' [Fr. Loftus was joined by two other visiting priests.] 'Oooh,' Katie said, 'That's Fr. Loftus—mother's great friend.' Ann replied, 'I knew the minute I came in this door that *he* was the one.'"

Katie and Ann sat next to each other during dinner, and afterward, Katie told Fr. Loftus that Ann had expressed a desire to be baptized—giving meaning to her comment, "He's the one." Fr. Loftus then discussed this news with June, making clear, "You just can't baptize anyone off the street." So June reassured him she would make the necessary arrangements, including an initial visit and formation in the faith.

In early December, he went over to Ann's house to talk with her. "There were four million things everywhere—mementos of one thing or another," he said. After breaking the ice, they had a "long chat," he said, during which she made clear, "She had always wanted to be a Catholic, it was in her heart." She would be spending Christmas at her place in Sedona, Arizona, after which June arranged for Fr. Loftus to give her a few "little talks" to explain the tenets of the faith. "At her age," he said, "there was no point in going into a big theology or anything." Then, he would baptize her at a mass at St. Mel's—"so that everybody would see it."

"So that was the plan," said Fr. Loftus.

Nothing went according to plan. No sooner had Ann returned from Sedona than she fell and was admitted to Cedars-Sinai Hospital in Beverly Hills. In her call to Fr. Loftus, reporting this turn of events, June said Ann would be out in two or three days, "so we better get working on it."

Meantime, providentially, Fr. Loftus had been invited to attend a big fundraising dinner for St. John of God, a rest home for elderly in downtown L.A., where he said Mass. They had a "terrible problem" that needed resolving, he said. Bishop Clark was coming to the dinner and, they said, "We have nobody to talk to him." Pleading with him to come to the dinner, he hesitated, given his other engagement. But they were insistent. So he said he would at least talk with the other host—the O'Neals, Marlene and Bob, producer of *Murder, She Wrote*. After explaining the situation, Marlene said, "Look, you better go to that. They need you. You can come here anytime. Don't worry about it; go."

On the way to the fundraising dinner at the Beverly Wilshire, Fr. Loftus thought, "Why don't I slip in to visit Ann in the hospital?" So he drove up to the hospital and scooted up to her room, intending just to say hello.

The minute he walked in, one of her assistants said, "Oh, Monsignor is here, oh, he'll baptize you now." What was immediately apparent, he said, was how "extremely weak" she was, leading him to conclude, "She's not coming out of the hospital."

"I had a nice visit with her," he said, during which his initial impression was reinforced, and he began thinking, "maybe she's dying." Concluding there was no time for "little talks," he said, "Ann, I'm going to baptize you *now*." Then, he "got the water, just blessed it, and gave her the simplest form of Baptism."

As he was heading out the door to go to the Beverly Wilshire, he said, "she looked out of the bed—she was very small you know—and said, 'Thank you, Father,' in a weak voice," with great reverence, which he imitated in the same soft voice in which she spoke.

Before leaving, he gave her secretary the phone number to his private room at St. Mel's to call him if anything happened. En route to the Beverly Wilshire he phoned June Haver to let her know he had baptized Ann, telling her, "She's extremely weak, she's not coming out of that hospital, so we need to get working." (She was dying of lung cancer.)

When he arrived back home from the dinner at about eleven o'clock, there was a message waiting for him that said, "Come in immediately. She's taken a turn."

"So, I turned back the car," he said, "and went straight into Cedars-Sinai, went up, and there she was." Though he was unsure whether or not she was conscious, he said, "I kept praying with her and talking to her and stayed there." He was planning to stay all night, if need be. But he would not be there long. "She died at thirty five after midnight, twenty five minutes to one," he said.

She was buried from St. Mel's. The funeral included all of her dance music played on the organ and several of her Hollywood friends' reminiscences. He remembered most vividly A.C. Lyles's eulogy. In it, he recalled, "Ann came to me and she said she met this priest at the Thanksgiving dinner and said, 'I want you to get a part for him in a movie. And, by the way, he comes with his own costume.'" Well, the church roared.

"God," said Fr. Loftus, "obviously wanted this for Ann before she died, because it was just miraculous." He had no idea how grave her situation was (June had said she'd be out of the hospital soon), and, but for the St. John of God engagement, he would not have been near the hospital, and she would have died without being baptized.

She had such joy on her face, he recalled, when she said, 'Thank you, Father.'" He believes those were her last words because, "very shortly after I left," he said, "she went into the coma." He knows that because they phoned right afterward to say she had taken a turn, a message he only received when he got home.

"God is always active, he never sleeps," Fr. Loftus summed up. "He's always doing things…this is our loving God. This is the way he works." With impeccable timing.

Chapter Thirteen

• • •

PATRICIA NEAL'S DRAMATIC
JOURNEY OF FAITH,
HEALING, AND FORGIVENESS

• • •

Time passes so quickly and we
endure so many crises—life, death,
and great, great pain.

—PATRICIA NEAL'S LETTER TO
VERONICA COOPER CONVERSE,
GARY COOPER'S WIDOW, IN 1981

"She was the best friend I ever had," Mother Dolores Hart said of
Patricia Neal, with a hint of that unforgettable Neal intonation.[1]

Neal was one of the twentieth century's most gifted actresses of
stage and screen, big and small, known for *Breakfast at Tiffany's*
(1961), *The Day the Earth Stood Still* (1951), and *Hud* (1963).
Yet, her life was often compared to a Greek tragedy. While
winning accolades for her acting prowess including a Best Actress
Oscar, a Tony, three Emmy nominations, and savoring her greatest
joy—that of mothering six children—she endured long periods of
intense personal pain. During a period of discontent, she went
to the Abbey of Regina Laudis in Bethlehem, Connecticut, at
the suggestion of Maria Cooper Janis, daughter of Gary Cooper
and longtime friend of Dolores Hart, now a cloistered nun at
the abbey. There she secured her single greatest achievement: a
surpassing quality of love, guided by the healing salve of forgiveness and spiritual richness of the Catholic faith.

From the Heart of the South

Patricia Neal—christened Patsy Louise—was born on January 20, 1926, in the small town of Packard, Kentucky, a close-knit community in the heart of coal country, where neighbor looked after neighbor and life's pleasures were simple.

"Life in Packard," she writes in her celebrated 1988 autobiography *As I Am*, "was very good." The hub of activity was the church—"of course, Baptist"—and general store.[2]

Her larger-than-life father William Burdette "Coot" Neal was from southern Virginia, where his family owned a tobacco plantation near Danville. Her earnest, warm-hearted mother, Eura Mildred Petrey, was from Packard, where her father, "Pappy," was the town doctor.[3]

"Remember what the psalmist says," Pappy would remind his granddaughter. "He changes desert into pools of water.'"[4]

The female preacher at Magnolia Avenue Methodist Church made an indelible impression on young Patsy during a revival meeting. "God is not keeping score...God is love," she said, draped in a long flowing white gown. "I had never been talked to about God like that," Patricia writes. Later that night, she gave up God for a cigarette and "felt so guilty."[5]

A Flair for Acting and Desire for Love

She exhibited her dramatic flair early on, giving her "first public performance" during an afternoon baseball game after studying *Julius Caesar* in the morning. Her sister, NiNi, pitching the ball, hit her face and, her nose gushing blood, she fell down, declaring Julius Caesar-like, "I am dead. I am dead."[6] Later, seeing "a glorious lady giving monologues," she realized, "that's all I wanted to do."[7] Now living in Knoxville, Tennessee, her parents signed her up for drama lessons on Christmas 1937, with the boss's daughter, who was back from New York. "My monologues," she writes, "graduated from the front yard to Aunt Maude's drawing room, and my audiences were growing. I got great notices the first play I did, so I knew I wanted to be an actress."[8] Soon she got a summer apprenticeship at Robert Porterfield's well-known Barter Theatre, where Depression era patrons bartered for tickets, and she even moved to New York for a time, meeting famed actress Katharine Cornell.

But her family rescued her, and it was off to Northwestern University. During her first year there, her "daddy"—"the rock upon which anything good about me has been built"—died of a heart attack.[9] Though eager to move to New York, she studied another year at Northwestern, at her family's urging, and managed to advance theatrically under the tutelage of drama teacher Alvina Krause, who was starting a summer theater and brought her along. From there, she headed for New York, where she quickly landed an understudy role in *The Voice of the Turtle* and, along with it, her new name—"Patricia," which the producer Alfred de Liagre thought matched her regal manner.[10]

"Applause," she writes, "was love. It was approval by everybody. And I bathed in it."[11]

She also wanted the real thing. In New York, at age nineteen, when her first boyfriend, the son of a doctor who procured abortions, told her he loved her more than anyone else, she traded in her virginity for love. When he dumped her for his virginal high school sweetheart, she was deeply wounded.[12]

Trusting her well-formed, sensitive theatrical instincts, she soon made her artistic mark, landing a starring role in *Another Part of the Forest* (1946) by Lillian Hellman, for which she won a Tony in the first such awards ceremony. At the same time, hardened in love, she pursued romance without conscience and wrecked two marriages.

As the film offers started pouring in, she landed a contract with Warner Bros. and the starring role in *John Loves Mary* (1949) opposite Ronald Reagan, whom she met on New Year's Eve 1947, upon arriving in Hollywood.

A year later, director King Vidor introduced her to Gary Cooper, as she tested for *The Fountainhead* (1949). She got the part and began a legendary affair with her married costar after filming wrapped.

"When the young doctor took my virginity and made me a bad woman," she writes, "I made up my mind I would never get hurt like that again…. Gary touched my heart as no one else had done before. I was really in love, and it was like I was innocent again."[13]

Predictably, the affair brought turmoil to everyone involved. After Patricia aborted the child she conceived with Coop, "she never had a day's peace thinking about that," said Mother Dolores—"why she did not have that child, why she was so stupid not to keep that child."[14] After the affair came to an end, as it had to, by Christmas 1951, she had a nervous breakdown. The Cooper family, too, suffered the strain of a temporary separation— Maria, as a child, famously spitting on Patricia in public.[15] "Gary adored her," Patricia writes.[16] And, "he loved Rocky," she told Robert Osbourne.

The bitterness would linger. In 1959—shortly after Patricia had seen Coop in London filming *The Wreck of the Mary Deare*, the last time she would see him—Maria glowered at her from afar during a chance encounter in New York. Rocky had given her the same look at a Jack Warner dinner party around 1951—"a laser beam," Patricia writes, signaling "'you really are a slut. You really are." The message was clear. "I did not dismiss the terrible guilt I felt. Our souls locked horns in a combat that would become the coldest of wars for the next 30 years."[17]

Soon thereafter, during a junket to Uruguay and Argentina for Warner Bros., June Haver "gave me my first taste of the Catholic Church," Patricia writes, inviting her to masses in the big cathedrals—"territory forbidden me as a child."[18] While there, Haver presented Eva (Evita) Peron with a crucifix.

Patricia began tasting more of the cross, as well, when Warner Bros.'s failed to renew her contract because of her affair, leaving her scrambling. She landed at Fox in a starring role in the sci-fi classic *The Day the Earth Stood Still* (1951). But it was not enough to salvage her tarnished career, and in 1951, she left Hollywood's "disappointments and heartaches" and returned to New York to star in Lillian Hellman's *The Children's Hour.*

Marriage and Family, Success and Tragedy

At a dinner party Hellman hosted, she met and would soon fall in love with renowned writer Roald Dahl, whom she married on July 2, 1953. The marriage had some initial bumps—Roald asking for a divorce the first year given his hurt male ego—Patricia was successful, he was not. But, crisis averted, their children began making their grand entrances—Olivia Twenty, born on April 20, 1955; Chantal Tessa Sophia, born on April 11, 1957; and Theo Matthew Roald, born on July 30, 1960—and Roald started thriving as a writer of children's books.

Their joy soon turned to sorrow when on December 5, 1960, their son Theo, just four months old, was struck by a taxi as the family au pair was strolling him along a New York City street. He suffered brain damage, occasioning many surgeries and the family's move back to England.

As Theo recovered, aided by Roald's development of a therapeutic intervention, both career and family life blossomed anew: Patricia played Mrs. Failenson in *Breakfast at Tiffany's* (1961), and they continued settling into a marvelous life in their white cottage with plush gardens at Great Missenden, not far from London, as, charmingly, Roald began testing his stories out on his children, and writing hits.

The following year, Olivia, not qualifying for a scarce measles vaccine, contracted and died of the disease on November 17, 1962. Roald was utterly devastated. As they gradually picked up the pieces, Patricia landed the role of Alma Brown in *Hud* (1963), for which she won the Best Actress Oscar—the director Martin Ritt kindly scheduling filming in segments so she could take care of her family.

A year later, Ophelia Magdalena was born on May 12, 1964, after which Patricia returned to work in early 1965, to make John Ford's *Seven Women*. She was once again pregnant (a fact known only to her and Roald), and one evening, home from the set, Roald, as usual, prepared her a martini after which she went up to bathe Tessa. A few minutes later, while lathering her baby down, she suffered three burst cerebral aneurysms.

It was February 17, 1965. Only thirty-nine, she was in a coma for three weeks. When she came to, she was a wreck. "I was as one dead," she writes. "My right side was completely paralyzed and I had been left with maddeningly double vision. I had not power of speech and my mind just didn't work."[19]

"At first I joked about suicide," she writes. "But I had begun to think about it. Everything had been stripped away. Roald was convinced depression I was feeling was due to worry and strain of carrying the baby. At first it gave me hope, now it was holding me back."[20]

As she struggled to conquer the blues, one day, the postman brought her a letter, the envelope to which was "inscribed with noble hand." It was from Maria Cooper. While her husband later burned it along with other materials on her desk, she could never forget the key sentence in Maria's letter. "I forgive you."[21] "The grace of God in Maria" is what prompted this gesture, Mother Dolores told EWTN's *The World Over*. "Maria knew that forgiveness demands an action...one of the deepest realities of Christian love."

It did Patricia a world of good and soon thereafter, on August 4, 1965, she gave birth to her baby girl, Lucy Neal.

Healing and faith

"Suddenly Patricia Neal wanted to live," *Life* magazine blared in its feature about her on November 15, 1965. Patricia countered, it would be truer to say, "Suddenly I realized I was, in fact, living and was starting to like the experience again."[22]

Valerie Eaton Griffith, her tutor, helped lift her "out of the cabbage patch," she writes. "A master can tell you what he expects...a teacher though awakens your own expectations."[23] Griffith helped her prepare for her first debut speech, made at The Waldorf Astoria in New York in March 1966, just over a year after losing all power of speech and mobility. Billed as "An Evening with Patricia Neal," for which she practiced to a wearying degree, it was a signal achievement for someone who had had to learn how to walk and speak again—and, perhaps, most dauntingly for an actress—remember lines.

As she basked in the applause, she writes, "I knew my life had been given back to me for one reason." Unsure what it was at the time, she credited "Roald the Rotten" for throwing her back into the deep water "where I belonged." "Tennessee hillbillies don't conk that easy," she writes.[24]

By 1967, she was cast in the lead for *The Subject Was Roses* (1968). While it was difficult to learn lines, she writes, "I was a hit...just for being alive."[25] In fact, she was fabulous. As her daughter Ophelia said, her recovery showed "she was a gift to the world."[26]

Indeed, she was.

Her story—initially publicized in that *Life Magazine* article—not only served as an inspiration to stroke victims worldwide, but was also the impetus for new hospitals and centers springing up nationwide focused on helping stroke patients rehabilitate—including the Patricia Neal Rehabilitation Center in her hometown.[27]

However, her cancer and life rehabilitation begain to suffer some setbacks. When she won the starring role in the television pilot for *The Waltons* (1971), she was not chosen for the role in the actual TV series because executives worried her health would not bear up under the pressure. Nor did her marriage bear up and, in 1972, Roald secretly began an affair with Catholic divorcee Felicity Crosland, the London-based freelance coordinator for David Ogilvy's ad agency, who worked with Patricia filming commercials for Maxim.

"While I sold coffee in my beautiful brown dress (hand-picked by Felicity), she sat on the floor staring up at me, her eyes dewy with admiration. I thought, what a lovely girl," Patricia writes.[28] Felicity, or Liccy, as she was nicknamed, soon became a familiar face at the Dahl house. She lived in a flat in London near Albert Bridge and began taking over Patricia's turf without her realizing it.

In 1973, as her Knoxville High School thirtieth reunion approached and the Maxim campaign was percolating, Patricia found herself returning every three weeks to New York and used the opportunity to write to Maria Cooper, who replied, "I very much want to see you." Finally, after many attempts, Maria agreed to join Patricia for breakfast in her hotel suite and upon arriving, Patricia writes, "spread her arms open to me. She held me, and the years of emptiness between me and Gary was over." "An amazing grace," Patricia writes, occurred during that meeting as she realized for the first time since her stroke, its gift: "Somehow, a memory that once had the power to wound me now passed benignly through my head."[29]

The memory was also being set right. As Patricia writes, "Maria finally asked, 'Is it true that you were pregnant by my father?'" Patricia confirmed it, expressing sorrow she had not had the baby. "It's my loss, too," Maria said. "I'm the only one."

Before the meeting ended, Maria asked her to promise to write to her mother, now "Mrs. John Converse." When Patricia lamented she wouldn't know what to say, Maria said, "You will," then gave her the address and left.

In the summer of 1978, while in Nice, Switzerland, on tour with *The Passage* company, she once again ran into Maria, now married to internationally renowned pianist Byron Janis, also on tour. During their daily visits, Patricia did not breathe a word about her problems with Roald. "But Maria," Patricia writes, "was amazingly intuitive. She sensed my inner anguish and asked me about my faith in God. I told her I had been struggling deeply about God since my stroke. Believing in Him again was very diffi-cult after seeming to lose everything."[30]

As Mother Dolores recounted, she asked Maria, "'What am I going to do with myself?' who replied, 'You go see my friend at the abbey.' And she said, 'They'll kill me.' And Maria said, 'Don't think of that. Go there. They're friends of Gary's.'"[31]

"Yes, I found myself thinking, that is something I would really like to do—sometime," she writes. "And, I slipped it into my bank of thoughts."[32] Not giving it a second thought, "one day in early December," she writes, "I received a letter from [Maria]. In it was a letter from one of the sisters inviting me to visit."[33]

Finally, Patricia called Maria and asked about that abbey. She gave her the number and the name of her good friend, Dolores Hart, who had lived at the abbey in consecrated life for fifteen years. "Through grace," Maria said, "she was the one who picked up the phone and made the appointment and took herself to the abbey." Her role, she said, was to "give her the opportunity," but after that "it was Pat's party."[34]

But as the date of her scheduled visit neared, Patricia writes, "I suddenly wondered what the hell I was doing, going to a Catholic nunnery."[35]

When she arrived at the abbey in May 1979, she writes, "I was taken to have a parlor with the nun who had written to me. She greeted me from behind a grille and had the most beautiful eyes I had ever seen." She outlined the plan for the three-day visit, and in response to Patricia's query about smoking told her, "while it was a 'prohibiting law,' the abbess 'knew from real sin,' and she was sure a way to indulge my vice could be found."

During prayers in the monastery chapel, "filled with flowers beautifully arranged...[and] calming strains of Gregorian chant...

from behind a large grille...." Patricia writes, "I remember thinking it was the first time I had felt close to peace in a long time." To top it off, the meals, she writes, were wonderful, especially the fresh bread, and she thoroughly enjoyed the other guest, a lovely Jewish woman named Sunny.

On the second day, she writes, "I worked up courage to talk about the struggle my marriage had become." The nun with the beautiful eyes only listened.

Later, a reading of Helen Keller she did for the abbey illuminated her path: "At other times," Keller writes, "things that I have been taught...and learned...drop away, as the lizard sheds its skin, and I see my soul as God sees it."

On the third day, the nun took her to the garden and "carefully avoided mentioning the affair with Gary," Patricia writes, except for noting, "I would have to go...even further back than the stroke to find the seeds of my discontent." The affair with Gary Cooper came spilling out. Patricia lamented "there was no way we could have been together." Au contraire, the nun said. She could remain close spiritually. It was a conversation Patricia "never forgot."

Before she left, Patricia chose a flower from the greenhouse as a remembrance of Olivia, which they "placed right in front of the altar." Seeing that, she returned to her "little room and wept." Later, while packing, she saw "the booze" she had brought to survive the whole experience. She had forgotten all about it. "An immediate blessing" followed her visit, she writes—"a good role in the television version of *All Quiet on the Western Front*" shot in Poland along with the consolation of Roald "remember[ing] to send me two divine bunches of flowers" on their wedding anniversary, the day she arrived home, even though he was in the hospital for another back operation.

The couple, she writes, ended the 1970s "with a bang of sorts," when Roald's rudeness at the Curzon Club, got him kicked out— his membership revoked forever. But the 1980s started on a better note, when, on a return trip to America, she visited the abbey and then, joined by Lucy and Ophelia, Martha's Vineyard, which she "fell in love with." It was "their first vacation without Papa." Later, Theo joined the threesome, and they visited California. While there, Patricia stopped by to see her old stand-in from Warner Bros. days, Ann Urcan, who had also suffered a stroke, now unable to speak or walk. "I told her I loved her and her eyes filled with tears."

"I was visiting my nunnery regularly, now, at least every three months," she writes. "I felt so comfortable there. I vaguely remembered my wonder at the peace June Haver had seemed to find in churches and nunneries in South America all those years ago. I was finding that same comfort." ("Comfortare," the sister had told me, meant "to make strong...the spirit of God, the life-giving flow of love.")[36]

Her life continued to change in other ways, as well, also to her great comfort. In February 1981, she happened to see the death notice for Rocky's second husband, Dr. John Marquis Converse, when she was in New York for *Ghost Story* (1981) location filming and was moved to finally fulfill the promise she made to Maria years earlier. She wrote to Rocky, and Maria told Patricia her mother was so moved that she read her letter "over and over." Amazingly, Rocky wrote her back on April 20, "my Olivia's birthday," said Patricia.[37]

"After some time had passed," Maria said, "she and my mother arranged to meet." That they became friends after years of acrimony was "so good," Patricia told Osbourne. "It's what life's made of." She needed that emotional shoring up. By Christmas 1982, "Mr. Roald Dahl," Mother Dolores said, "threw her out of her home, laughingly—laughing, 'Get out of here you tramp.' He just took her to an airport and put her on a plane and said just get out of my life, get out of the country."[38]

As 1983 opened up, Patricia, devastated and angry, came to the States intent on writing a scathing autobiography. "Mother Benedict Duss took her up to the tower," said Mother Dolores, and they discussed the matter, as follows:

"Patricia, my friend, you are not going to write this book about Roald Dahl that's in you."

"How do you know that?"

"Because Dolores told me. I'm telling you, you're not going to do it because you cannot spread further ugliness. It will never help you. You will never get better. You stay here."

"How can I stay here?"

"Why don't you become a pre-postulant for a couple of months? Just put on this dress, you know. Say you're trying it out. Nobody will bother you. Believe me. It's so quiet."

"Patricia came and she was the best duster we ever had," Mother Dolores said. "She dusted everything." Unsurprisingly, the Lady Abbess secretly wished "she could stay," said Mother Dolores. "But then Patricia left to find out how she was going to get her life back."[39]

Mother Dolores reached out for help to her good friend, Dick DeNeut, whose idea was to make a film with Patricia playing Anastasia to build her confidence. But she said, "In the final analysis, Lady Abbess told Patricia, 'Mother Dolores will help you write the book.' 'Yes, well, what shall I do?" Mother Dolores wondered, to which she replied, "Sit there with the typewriter, you listen to everything she says and write it down." Well, Mother Dolores said, with humor, "I have 1200 pages of Patricia Neal." After that, she pondered the gargantuan task of shaping it into a book and getting it published and again called DeNeut, who offered to edit it, transforming it into *As I Am.*

The abbey would be a continuing source of solace and strength for Patricia, who "came back all of her life, she found a way"— for instancing coming "every time we had a fair to sell her book," said Mother Dolores.

One day, she "finally said to me, 'You know, I'm going to become a Catholic before I die. It will just be when I die.' I said, 'You can't do that to God.' And she said, 'Why can't I do that to God?'" which Mother Dolores recounted, imitating that husky, expressive voice of hers.

"It was about a day before she died that she converted," said Mother Dolores.

"She was one of the most fantastic persons on screen," Mother Dolores said, citing *Hud.* Patricia explained her technique, saying, "You don't think about it. You just do it. Don't even worry about it. You just know what to do and it comes to you."

In 1990, shortly before Theo turned thirty, Patricia finally decided to call Roald and Felicity, now married, and let bygones be bygones. She talked to Roald three more times before his death later that year. November 17 was "the last time I hung up on my love," she writes—coincidentally the anniversary of Olivia's death as well as that of his mother.

On August 8, 2010, Patricia Neal died of lung cancer at age eighty-four in her beloved Martha's Vineyard and was laid to rest at the Abbey of Regina Laudis, according to her wishes. "At her burial," Mother Dolores said, "a group of her buddies bade her farewell singing "Luck Be a Lady."

"She wanted to be buried at the abbey and so her grave is in the abbey cemetery right next to my grandmother and my mother's," said Mother Dolores of her "best friend."[40]

Maria Cooper Janis, Mother Dolores Hart, and Patricia Neal at the Neuropathy Association's 2004 "Intimate Evening" Gala

Conclusion

"It's a nightmare out there! It hurts what we do in our private lives," said Betty Hutton.[1] These stories affirm her words. But as each star's journey reveals, it's possible to recover—and faith is a powerful force in that recovery.

Of course, the power and force of Hollywood's lifestyle—the talent, the stardom, the celebrity, the money, and all the luxury that goes along with it—are hard to counteract and these stories are, fittingly, dramatic in the telling of that effort.

But, in spite of all the glamour, they were just ordinary humans, after all—with the same everyday concerns and desires, like everyone else, and easy prey to the same pitfalls and in need of the same help from God.

Only, their stories played out larger.

Dramatic falls, in many cases, and dramatic rescues all.

In the end, just as they were so generous with their talents, so, too, was God with his grace, showering it abundantly to help them discover the key to happiness lies not in the dreams Hollywood manufactures, but in the true joy that comes only from God, which, as St. Josemaria Escriva de Balaguer always said, "has its roots in the form of a cross."[2] "True joy," which, as St. Francis famously said, "would not consist in doing a lot of miracles," but rather in "remaining patient and not getting upset" after being treated poorly.[3]

Imagine if a wave of patience and calm washed over Hollywood, if not the world. This book, these stories of sufferng—what the Latin word *patientia* (i.e., patience) means—illumine the way.

Bibliography

CHAPTER ONE

Barrymore, Ethel. *Memories*. London: Hulton, 1956.

Basinger, Jeanine. *Silent Stars*. New York: Alfred A. Knopf, 1999.

Beauchamp, Cari. *Joseph Kennedy Presents: His Hollywood Years*. New York: Alfred A. Knopf, 2009.

Cary, Gary. *Doug & Mary: A Biography of Douglas Fairbanks & Mary Pickford*. New York: E.P. Dutton, 1977.

Chang, David A.Y.O. "Spencer Tracy's Boyhood: Truth, Fiction and Hollywood Dreams." Wisconsin: *Wisconsin Magazine of History*, Autumn 2000.

Curtis, James. *Spencer Tracy, A Biography*. New York: Alfred A. Knopf, 2011.

Davidson, Bill. *Spencer Tracy: Tragic Idol*. New York: E.P. Dutton, 1987.

Kanin, Garson. *Tracy and Hepburn: An Intimate Memoir*. New York: Viking, 1971.

CHAPTER TWO: ALFRED HITCHCOCK

Gervasi, Sacha. *Hitchcock*. Los Angeles: Fox Searchlight Pictures, 2012.

Henninger, Mark. "Alfred Hitchcock's Surprise Ending." *Wall Street Journal*, December 6, 2012.

McGilligan, Patrick. *Alfred Hitchcock: A Life in Darkness and Light*. New York: Harper Collins, 2003.

Spoto, Donald. *The Dark Side of Genius: The Life of Alfred Hitchcock*. Boston: Little, Brown, 1983.

Taylor, John Russell. *Hitch: The Life and Times of Alfred Hitchcock*. New York: Pantheon, 1978.

CHAPTER THREE: GARY COOPER

Portions of this chapter appeared in "Gary Cooper's Authenticity," published in *National Catholic Register* on July 21, 2011. Portions of this chapter were also previously published in *Forbes*, available online at http://www.forbes.com/sites/maryclairekendall/2013/05/13/gary-coopers-quiet-journey-of-faith/.

Janis, Maria Cooper. *Gary Cooper Off Camera: A Daughter Remembers*. New York: Abrams, 1999.

Barry, Norman. *The Hollywood Greats*. London: Franklin Watts, 1980.

Hotchner, A.E. *Papa Hemingway.* New York: Random House, 1955.

Meyers, Jeffrey. *Gary Cooper: American Hero*. New York: Morrow, 1998.

McBride, Joseph. *Frank Capra: The Catastrophe of Success*. New York: Simon & Schuster, 1992.

Waterbury, Ruth. "The Real Reason Gary Cooper Became a Catholic." *Motion Picture Magazine*, November 1959.

CHAPTER FOUR: BOB HOPE

Hope, Bob, and Linda Hope. *My Life in Jokes*. New York: Hyperion, 2003.

———— with Pete Martin. *Have Tux, Will Travel: Bob Hope's Own Story*. New York: Simon and Schuster, 1954.

Hope, Bob, with Melville Shavelson. *Don't Shoot, It's Only Me*. New York: G.P. Putnam's Sons, 1990.

Marx, Arthur. *The Secret Life of Bob Hope, An Unauthorized Biography*. New York: Barricade, 1993.

Stephen M. Silverman. "Dolores Hope, Widow of Bob Hope, Dies. *People*, September 19, 2011.

Zoglin, Richard. *Hope: The Untold Story of Bob Hope, the Most Important Entertainer of the Twentieth Century*. New York: Simon and Schuster, 2014.

CHAPTER FIVE: MARY ASTOR

Astor, Mary. *A Life in Film*. New York: Delacorte, 1967.

————. *My Story: An Autobiography*. Doubleday, 1959.

————. "What I have learned about the Gift of Faith." New York: *Guideposts*, July 1959.

"Cinema: Rags & Riches." *Time Magazine*, Monday, April 2, 1934.

CHAPTER SIX: JOHN WAYNE

Eyman, Scott. *John Wayne: Life and Legend*. New York: Simon and Schuster, 2014.

Hepburn, Katherine. "Hooked on John Wayne." *TV Guide*, September 17, 1977.

Medley, Tony. "Patrick Wayne Reflects on John Wayne as a Father." www.tonymedley.com, 2012.

Wayne, John. *Disney Magazine*, February 1977.

CHAPTER SEVEN: ANN SOTHERN

Briggs, Colin. *Cordially Yours, Ann Sothern*. Albany, Ga.: Bear Manor, 2007.

Harmetz, Aljean. "Ann Sothern Dauntless." *New York Times*, October 11, 1987.

———. "Ann Sothern Is Dead at 92; Savvy Star of B-Films and TV." *New York Times*, March 17, 2001.

"The New Pictures." *Time Magazine*, October 18, 1943.

CHAPTER EIGHT: JANE WYMAN

Morris, Edmund. *Dutch: A Memoir of Ronald Reagan*. New York: Random House, 1999.

"Jane Wyman Divorced." *The New York Times*, March 10, 1965.

Kendall, Mary Claire. "How Jane Wyman Dealt with Tragedy." *Forbes*, 2013. http://www.forbes.com/sites/maryclairekendall/2013/01/05/how-jane-wyman-dealt-with-tragedy/.

Reagan, Michael. *Twice Adopted*. Nashville: Broadman & Holman, 2004.

Vallance, Tom. Jane Wyman obituary. *The Independent* (London), September 11, 2007.

CHAPTER NINE: SUSAN HAYWARD

Anderson, Christopher. *A Star, Is A Star, Is A Star! The Lives and Loves of Susan Hayward*. Garden City, N.Y.: Doubleday, 1980.

Linet, Beverly. *Portrait of a Survivor: Susan Hayward*. New York: Atheneum, 1980.

Susan Hayward: Brooklyn Bombshell. A&E Biography, 1996.

CHAPTER TEN: LANA TURNER

Basinger, Jeanine. *The Star Machine*. New York: Vintage, 2009.

"Lana Turner's Last Interview - Part 1." YouTube video, 5:59. From *Lifestyles of the Rich and Famous*, September 1994. Posted by falconcrestblog, Januaray 2, 2010, https://www.youtube.com/watch?v=mnvSy8gEF4I.

"Lana Turner's Last Interview - Part 2." YouTube video, 5:59. From *Lifestyles of the Rich and Famous*, September 1994. Posted by falconcrestblog, Januaray 2, 2010, https://www.youtube.com/watch?v=K5om-dbir0A.

Turner, Lana. *Lana: The Lady, the Legend, the Truth*. New York: E.P Dutton, 1982.

CHAPTER ELEVEN: BETTY HUTTON

I have written about Betty Hutton for *Our Sunday Visitor* in a piece titled, "Priest and Eucharist helped actress find herself," in May 2007 http://www.maryclairecinema.com/pubs/ Betty%20Hutton%20feature%20(OSV)%205-27-07.pdf; *Newport Life Magazine*, in a piece titled, "Being Beautiful Betty," in May 2009; *National Catholic Register* in December 2011; and *Forbes*, in a piece titled "Betty Hutton's Miraculous Recovery," in March 2013 http://www.forbes.com/sites/maryclairekendall/2013/03/11/betty-huttons-miraculous-recovery/.

Christy, Marian. "Betty Hutton: I'm A Phoenix." *The Boston Globe*, December 10, 1986.

"Command Performance Strictly G.I. Part 1 of 2." YouTube video, 7:39. Posted by Historycomestolife, July 5, 2010, https://www.youtube.com/watch?v=1YNRgO5vlQ4.

Hutton, Betty, with Carl Bruno and Michael Mayer. *Backstage You Can Have*. Palm Springs, Calif.: The Betty Hutton Estate, 2009.

Hutton, Betty. Interview by Mike Douglas. *The Mike Douglas Show*, February 25, 1977.

Judge, Jean. "Ageless Betty Hutton: She's 'right up front.'" *Herald News*, Tuesday, September 21, 1982.

Krieger, Elliott. "Betty Hutton Receives Degree at Salve Regina." *Providence Journal Bulletin*, September 30, 1984

Osbourne, Robert "Private Screenings with Betty Hutton." Interview by Turner Classic Movies, April 2000.

Polichetti, Barbara. "Betty Hutton Moves to the Head of the Class." *Providence Journal-Bulletin*, May 19, 1986.

Sharbutt, Jay. "Bombshell Betty Hutton hits Broadway in 'Annie.'" *Associated Press*, September 13, 1980.

"This Side of Happiness." *Time Magazine*, April 24, 1950.

The Betty Hutton Website. "About Betty"—Timeline. www.satin-sandspurs.com/biography.

Obituaries in *The Independent* (London), March 14, 2007; *The Telegraph*; March 14, 2007; and *The Desert Sun*, March 24, 2007.

CHAPTER TWELVE: ANN MILLER

Miller, Ann, and Norma Lee Browning. *Miller's High Life*. Garden City, N.Y.: Doubleday & Co., Inc., 1972.

CHAPTER THIRTEEN: PATRICIA NEAL

An earlier version of this story was published in *National Catholic Register* as well as in Forbes at http://www.forbes.com/sites/mary-clairekendall/2013/08/08/patricia-neals-dramatic-journey-of-love-healing-forgiveness/ on the first and second anniversaries of her death, respectively.

"Private Screenings with Patricia Neal." Interview by Robert Osbourne. Turner Classic Movies, April 2004.

Shearer, Stephen Michael. *Patricia Neal: An Unquiet Life.* Lexington, Ky.: The University Press of Kentucky.

Neal, Patricia, and Richard DeNeut. *As I Am: An Autobiography.* New York: Simon and Schuster, 1988.

Notes

DEDICATION

Lillian's mother, Martha Mungen Starrett (1837–1881), grew up on Harrison Plantation on Amelia Island, near Jacksonville, Florida. She met Bradshaw Hall Webster (1836–1889) of Orono, Maine, when he was campaigning with Abe Lincoln fresh out of college and they married soon thereafter. Union troops destroyed Harrison Plantation in 1862, and nearly twenty years later, in 1881, after Martha died, Bradshaw, a thirty-third degree Mason married a Catholic named "Annie," whom he met through the convent school in Birmingham, Alabama, where he sent Lillian, aged three, during the summers. He chose this school, Lillian wrote in her diary, because the nuns, including Annie's sister Stella, "taught the girls how to be ladies."

INTRODUCTION

1. A.E. Hotchner, *Papa Hemingway* (New York: Random House, 1955), p. x.

CHAPTER ONE

1. Bruce Marshall, *The World, the Flesh and Father Smith* (New York: Houghton Mifflin, 1945), p. 108.
2. Bob Thomas, Associated Press, March 13, 2007.
3. Jeanine Basinger, *Silent Stars* (New York: Alfred A. Knopf, 1999), p. 18.
4. Basinger, *Silent Stars*, p. 7.
5. *Mary Pickford: A Life on Film*, Timeline Films and the Mary Pickford Foundation.
6. *Mary Pickford: A Life on Film*.
7. Basinger, *Silent Stars*, p. 4.
8. Gary Cary, *Doug & Mary: A Biography of Douglas Fairbanks & Mary Pickford* (New York: E.P Dutton, 1977), pp. 76–79.
9. Cary.
10. Cary, pp. 99–100.
11. Cari Beauchamp, *Joseph Kennedy Presents: His Hollywood Years* (New York: Alfred A. Knopf, 2009), p. 110.
12. *Swanson on Swanson*, by Gloria Swanson, page 61.
13. Beauchamp, pp. 120–135.
14. Beauchamp, p. 134.

15. Beauchamp, p. 107.

16. Ethel Barrymore, *Memories* (London: Hulton, 1956), pp. 14.

17. Barrymore, pp. 18–19.

18. Barrymore, pp. 18–19.

19. Barrymore, pp. 27–28.

20. Barrymore, p. 126.

21. Barrymore, p. 132.

22. Barrymore, p. 130. A young colleague, Frank McIntyre, who took his work more seriously, was nurtured by one of the partners, Mr. O'Keefe, who finding out he had a vocation to be a priest, "helped him through a theological seminary," she wrote.

23. Barrymore, p. 136.

24. Barrymore, pp. 213.

25. Barrymore, p. 214.

26. Barrymore, p. 218.

27. Barrymore, p. 26.

28. Bill Davidson, *Spencer Tracy: Tragic Idol* (New York: E.P. Dutton, 1987), p. 12.

29. In those days, it was not uncommon for a young man to enter the seminary, at the least, to eliminate the possibility he had a priest's vocation, considered the highest calling. My own grandfather, Frank Biberstein, also born in 1900, attended Charles Borromeo seminary in Philadelphia for a time.

30. "Spencer Tracy's Boyhood: Truth, Fiction and Hollywood Dreams," *Wisconsin Magazine of History*, Autumn 2000, p. 32.

31. Garson Kanin, *Tracy and Hepburn: An Intimate Memoir* (New York: Viking, 1971), p. 14.

32. *Theater Arts Magazine*, February 1960.

33. Perhaps he added this in at the last minute, because it is not in the record of his Washington, D.C., visit. However, a week before, he told the youth of Ireland the same thing, beautifully so, when he said, "In Christ you will discover the true greatness of your own humanity."

Chapter Two

1. Donald Spoto, *The Dark Side of Genius: The Life of Alfred Hitchcock* (Boston: Little, Brown, 1983), p. 18.

2. Fr. Mark Henninger, interview with the author, May 28, 2014.

3. Fr. Mark Henninger, "Alfred Hitchcock's Surprise Ending," *Wall Street Journal*, December 6, 2012.

4. Fr. Mark Henninger, "Alfred Hitchcock's Surprise Ending."

5. Henninger, interview.

6. Henninger, "Alfred Hitchcock's Surprise Ending."

7. Patrick McGilligan, *Alfred Hitchcock: A Life in Darkness and Light* (New York: Harper Collins, 2003), p. 89.

8. McGilligan, p. 7.

9. McGilligan, p. 6.

10. McGilligan, p. 15.

11. McGilligan, p. 6.

12. John Russell Taylor, *Hitch: The Life and Times of Alfred Hitchcock* (New York: Pantheon, 1968), p. 18.

13. McGilligan, p. 13.

14. McGilligan, p. 24.

15. Henninger, interview.

16. Taylor, p. 33.

17. McGilligan, p. 28.

18. McGilligan, p. 54.

19. Taylor, p. 18.

20. Spoto, p. 552.

21. Henninger, interview.

22. McGilligan, p. 440.

23. Henninger, "Alfred Hitchcock's Surprise Ending."

24. Henninger, interview.

CHAPTER THREE

1. Maria Cooper Janis, *Gary Cooper Off Camera: A Daughter Remembers* (New York: Abrams, 1999), p. 49.

2. Jeffrey Meyers, *Gary Cooper: American Hero* (New York: Morrow, 1998), p. 110.

3. Maria Cooper Janis, interview with author, April 12, 2008.

4. Janis, interview.

5. A.C. Lyles, interview with author, July 2011.

6. Joseph McBride, *Frank Capra: The Catastrophe of Success* (New York: Simon and Schuster, 1992), p. 345.

7. "Gary Cooper Interview," YouTube video, 0:36, posted by SickerVideo,

October 10, 2009, https://www.youtube.com/watch?v=lKvJWsk-Jc8.

8. Meyers, pp. 250–251.

9. Meyers, p. 74.

10. Meyers, p. 206.

11. Janis, *Gary Cooper Off Camera*, pp. 64–66.

12. Janis, *Gary Cooper Off Camera*, p. 67.

13. Meyers, p. 206.

14. Janis, *Gary Cooper Off Camera*, p. 66.

15. Janis, *Gary Cooper Off Camera*, p. 79.

16. Janis, interview, April 12, 2008; and Janis, *Gary Cooper Off Camera*, p. 79.

17. Janis, *Gary Cooper Off Camera*, p. 84.

18. Janis, *Gary Cooper Off Camera*, p. 67.

19. Meyers, p. 277.

20. Janis, *Gary Cooper Off Camera*, p. 161.

21. Ruth Waterbury, "The Real Reason Gary Cooper Became a Catholic," *Motion Picture*, November 1959, p. 88.

22. Waterbury, p. 53.

23. Cooper visited the Soviet Union at the invitation of Nikita Khrushchev, who was favorably impressed by the star's humanity and warmth.

24. Maria Cooper Janis, interview with author, August 2012.

25. Meyers, p. 311.

26. Janis, *Gary Cooper Off Camera*, p. 98.

27. Janis, *Gary Cooper Off Camera*, p. 147.

28. Hotchner, p. 289.

29. Hotchner, p. 290.

30. "Cooper: I'm not afraid, It's God's will," *The Straits Times*, May 6, 1961.

31. Hemingway died of a self-inflicted gunshot wound on July 2, 1961, just six weeks after Cooper. He was suffering severe mental illness at the time.

CHAPTER FOUR

1. *People Magazine*, September 19, 2011; Richard Zoglin, "New Book Reveals Johnny Carson's Least Favorite Tonight Show Guest: Bob Hope," *People Magazine*, November 6, 2014, www.people.com/people/news/category/0,,personsTax:BobHope,00.html.

2. Bob Hope, with Pete Martin, *Have Tux, Will Travel: Bob Hope's Own Story* (New York: Simon and Schuster, 1954), p. 5.

3. *Guinness Book of World Records*, www.bobhope.com/guinness.htm.

4. Harry Flynn, interview with the author, May 29, 2013.

5. Hope, *Have Tux, Will Travel*, p. 14.

6. Hope, *Have Tux, Will Travel*, pp. 27–28.

7. Hope, *Have Tux, Will Travel*, p. 24.

8. Richard Zoglin, *Hope: The Untold Story of Bob Hope, the Most Important Entertainer of the Twentieth Century*, p. 38.

9. Hope, *Have Tux, Will Travel*, p. 43.

10. Hope, *Have Tux, Will Travel*, p. 45.

11. Hope, *Have Tux, Will Travel*, p. 65.

12. Hope, *Have Tux, Will Travel*, pp. 68–69.

13. Hope, *Have Tux, Will Travel*, p. 75.

14. "Bob Hope and American Variety: Vaudeville," Library of Congress, Exhibitions, www.loc.gov/exhibits/bobhope/vaude.html.

15. Hope did two more Broadway shows—*Ziegfeld Follies* (1936) and *Red Hot and Blue* (1937).

16. He did a benefit there, as well, for the Bob Hope Theater in Eltham in 1991.

17. Fr. Groeschel of the Franciscan Friars of the Renewal was a good friend of the Hopes, introduced by the Gallo family. I interviewed him in September 2011.

18. Hope, *Have Tux, Will Travel*, pp. 111–112.

19. Arthur Marx, *The Secret Life of Bob Hope* (New York: Barricade, 1993).

20. Zoglin, pages 94–97.

21. Marx, p. 301.

22. Marx, p. 18.

23. Zoglin, page 31.

24. Marx, p. 182.

25. Hope, *Have Tux, Will Travel*, p. 282.

26. Marx, p. 465.

27. Marx, p. 362.

28. Valerie J. Nelson, "Dolores Hope dies at 102; widow of Bob Hope," *Los Angeles Times*, September 19, 2011.

29. Zoglin, p. 445.

30. I experienced this firsthand, when I met Dolores Hope in March 1994 at St. Matthews Cathedral in Washington, D.C., and she asked me to "pray for Bob."

31. Dolores Hope to Fr. George Rutler, December 9, 1991, provided by Fr. George Rutler.

32. Bob Hope, with Linda Hope, *My Life in Jokes* (New York: Hyperion, 2003), p. 59.

33. Hope, *My Life in Jokes*, p. 199.

34. Marx, p. 467.

35. Bob Hope, with Melville Shavelson, *Don't Shoot, It's Only Me* (New York: Putnam, 1990), p. 13.

36. Marx, p. 470.

CHAPTER FIVE

1. Mary Astor, "What I Have Learned about the Gift of Faith," *Guideposts*, July 1959.

2. Astor, "What I Have Learned."

3. Mary Astor, *My Story: An Autobiography* (New York: Doubleday, 1959), p. 29.

4. Astor, *My Story*, pp. 34–35.

5. Astor, *My Story*, pp. 34–35.

6. Astor, *My Story*, p. 44.

7. Astor, *My Story*, pp. 44–45.

8. Astor, *My Story*, p. 45.

9. Astor, *My Story*, p. 46.

10. Astor, *My Story*, p. 47. Also applies to next paragraph's quotes.

11. Astor, *My Story*, p. 48.

12. "Cinema: Rags & Riches," *Time Magazine*, Monday, April 2, 1934. *Time* says the family moved to Chicago in 1917. Later sources cite 1919, which seems too compressed to accomplish all she supposedly did in 1919. Favoring 1917 is the fact that, as she writes, she was in her "sixth year," i.e., age eleven, or 1917, in Chicago. The one inconsistency is that Astor says the *Motion Picture Magazine* semi-finalist selection spurred the move to Chicago and that a year later she entered the contest again, occasioning the move to New York. This recollection favors 1919. But, other reporting says Otto moved the family to Chicago to teach

German. Research shows his German text was published in spring 1917 in Quincy, not 1914, as she writes. It's likely he moved to Chicago to teach German, after the publication of his book, and to be closer the film action. Reporting shows, he began entering Mary in contests in 1916. Then after his book failed, and teaching dried up, it's likely he began focusing solely on making Mary a star.

13. Astor, *My Story*, p. 49.
14. Astor, *My Story*, p. 49.
15. Astor, *My Story*, pp. 52–53.
16. Astor, *My Story*, p. 57.
17. Astor, *My Story*, p. 11.
18. Astor, *My Story*, pp. 74–76.
19. Western Association of Motion Picture Advertisers.
20. Astor, *My Story*, pp. 101–102.
21. Astor, *My Story*, p. 109.
22. Astor, *My Story*, p. 116.
23. Astor, *My Story*, p. 122.
24. Astor, *My Story*, p. 128.
25. Astor, *My Story*, pp. 129–130.
26. Astor, *My Story*, p. 137.
27. Astor, *My Story*, p. 146.
28. Astor, *My Story*, p. 161.
29. Mary Astor, *A Life in Film* (New York: Delacorte, 1967), p. 125.
30. Astor, "What I Have Learned."
31. St. Therese had said before she died, "I will spend my Heaven doing good on earth. I will let fall a shower of roses."
32. Astor, "What I Have Learned."
33. Astor, p. 208.
34. Astor, "What I Have Learned."
35. Astor, p. 211.
36. Astor, p. 191.
37. Astor, p. 250.
38. Astor, p. 253.
39. Astor, p. 254.
40. Her daughter said, becoming Catholic was one of her mother's stipulations for marrying Frank Roh. They wed on her eighteenth

birthday—June 15, 1950. She left the church nine years later.
41. Astor, p. 257.
42. Astor, p. 258.
43. Astor, pp. 258–259.
44. Astor, p. 260.
45. Astor, p. 261.
46. Astor, p. 264.
47. Astor, p. 312.
48. Astor, p. 312.
49. Astor, pp. 11–12.
50. Astor, p. 13.
51. Astor, pp. 17–18.
52. Astor, p. 18.
53. Astor, prologue, pp. 22–25.
54. Astor, pp. 22–25.
55. Astor, p. 25.
56. Astor, "What I Have Learned."
57. Astor, *A Life in Film*, p. 215.
58. Marylyn Roh, interview with author, March 30, 2014.

CHAPTER SIX
1. His middle name was changed to Mitchell when his younger brother, Robert, came along in December 1911. Scott Eyman, *John Wayne: Life and Legend* (New York: Simon and Schuster, 2014), pp. 15–16.
2. Eyman, p. 20.
3. John Wayne, "Can you judge a book by its cover?... Not according to Duke," *Disney Magazine* (February 1976).
4. His father remarried shortly after his divorce, and his situation stabilized, and he eventually rose to become head of the Beverly Hills Lyons Club.
5. Gretchen Wayne, interview with author, April 14, 2014; and a follow-up interview on June 2, 2014.
6. Eyman, p. 60.
7. Eyman, pp. 61–62.
8. Eyman, p. 69.
9. Eyman, p. 73.
10. Eyman, p. 98.

11. Eyman, p. 127.
12. Eyman, p. 114.
13. Eyman, p. 118.
14. Eyman, p. 120.
15. Eyman, p. 154.
16. Eyman, p. 224.
17. Eyman, p. 415.
18. Eyman, p. 229.
19. A.J. Fenady, interview with author, May 24, 2012.
20. Eyman, p. 428.
21. Katharine Hepburn, "Hooked on John Wayne," *TV Guide*, September 17, 1977.
22. Scott Eyman, p. 517.
23. Tony Medley, "Patrick Wayne Reflects on John Wayne as a Father," 2012 http://www.tonymedley.com/Articles/Patrick_Wayne_Reflects_on_John_Wayne_as_a_Father.htm
24. Medley, "Patrick Wayne Reflects."

CHAPTER SEVEN
1. Aljean Harmetz, "Ann Sothern Is Dead at 92; Savvy Star of B-Films and TV," *New York Times*, March 17, 2001.
2. Harmetz.
3. "The New Pictures," *Time*, October 18, 1943.
4. Harmetz.
5. Harmetz.
6. Colin Briggs, *Cordially Yours, Ann Sothern*, 2007, p. 135.
7. Harmetz.
8. Briggs, p. 138.
9. Harmetz.
10. Harmetz.
11. Harmetz.
12. Harmetz.

CHAPTER EIGHT
1. Mary Claire Kendall, "How Jane Wyman Dealt with Tragedy," *Forbes*, January 5, 2013, http://www.forbes.com/sites/maryclairekendall/2013/01/05/how-jane-wyman-dealt-with-tragedy/.

2. Jane Wyman obituary. *The Independent* (London), September 11, 2007.
3. Jane Wyman obituary.
4. Edmund Morris, *Dutch: A Memoir of Ronald Reagan* (New York: Random House, 1999), p. 153.
5. Morris, p. 154, undated interview clip preserved in State Historical Society of Wisconsin.
6. Morris, pp. 162.
7. Morris, pp. 162–163.
8. Jane Wyman obituary.
9. The film introduced the Oscar-winning Hoagy Carmichael and Johnny Mercer hit song, "In the Cool, Cool, Cool of the Evening," written for an unrealized musical based on the life of Mabel Normand intended as a Betty Hutton vehicle.
10. Jane Wyman obituary.
11. I first interviewed Virginia Zamboni in September 2007, shortly after the death of Jane Wyman, when I was writing an article for *Our Sunday Visitor*, and then in December 2011 when I was writing an article for *National Catholic Register*, and then a few times in the spring of 2014, while I was working on *Journeys of Faith, Lives of Hollywood Legends*.
12. Michael Reagan, *Twice Adopted* (Nashville: Broadman & Holman, 2004), p. 26.
13. "Jane Wyman Divorced," *The New York Times*, March 10, 1965.
14. I interviewed Fr. Howard Lincoln in September 2007, shortly after Jane Wyman's death, for an article I was writing for *Our Sunday Visitor*.

CHAPTER NINE
1. Christopher Anderson, *A Star, Is A Star, Is A Star! The Lives and Loves of Susan Hayward* (Garden City, N.Y.: Doubleday, 1980), p. 6.
2. Anderson, page 6.
3. Anderson, p. 7.
4. Anderson, p. 47.
5. Anderson, p. 49.
6. Anderson, p. 41.
7. Lucky Brown, interview with author, May 2014. His family were Hollywood founders, building the studio that later became Paramount.

8. Her friend, Patricia Morrison, said the event was the Biltmore, *A&E's Biography: Susan Hayward*. Christopher Anderson said it was the Ambassador Hotel.

9. Anderson, p. 61.

10. Anderson, p. 63.

11. Anderson, p. 73.

12. Anderson, pp. 87–88.

13. Kim Holston, *Susan Hayward: Her Life and Films*, p. 64.

14. Anderson, p. 126.

15. Beverly Linet, *Portrait of a Survivor: Susan Hayward* (New York: Atheneum, 1980), p. 147.

16. Linet, p. 180.

17. Linet, p. 211.

18. Linet, p. 219.

19. Anderson, p. 199.

20. Linet, p. 225.

21. Linet, p. 248.

22. Linet, p. 253.

23. Linet, p. 254.

24. The church was sold and closed in the early 1990s.

25. Linet, p. 272.

26. Linet, p. 250.

27. Linet, p. 274.

28. Linet, p. 286.

CHAPTER TEN

1. Lana Turner, *Lana: The Lady, the Legend, the Truth* (New York: E.P Dutton, 1982), p. 10.

2. Turner, pp. 12–13.

3. Turner, p. 13.

4. Turner, p. 13.

5. Turner, p. 16

6. Turner, pp. 16–17.

7. Turner, p. 16.

8. Turner, p. 17.

9. Turner, pp. 17–18.

10. Turner, pp. 18–19.

11. Turner, p. 25.

12. Turner, p. 26.

13. Turner, p. 28.

14. Jeanne Basinger, *The Star Machine* (New York: Vintage, 2009).

15. Turner, p. 34.

16. Turner, pp. 35–36.

17. Turner, p. 39.

18. Turner, p. 41.

19. Turner, pp. 43–47.

20. Turner, pp. 58–59.

21. Turner, pp. 64–66.

22. Turner, p. 67.

23. Turner, p. 75.

24. Turner, pp. 76, 79.

25. Turner, p. 81.

26. Turner, p. 82.

27. Turner, p. 137.

28. Turner, p. 233.

29. Turner, p. 248.

30. Turner, p. 251.

31. Turner, p. 260.

32. Turner, p. 294.

33. Turner, p. 306.

34. Turner, p. 307.

35. Turner, p. 81.

36. Turner, p. 147.

37. Her final interview, which Robin Leach conducted on *Lifestyles of the Rich and Famous*. "Lana Turner's Last Interview - Part 1." YouTube video, 5:59. From *Lifestyles of the Rich and Famous*, September 1994. Posted by falconcrestblog, Januaray 2, 2010, https://www.youtube.com/watch?v=mnvSy8gEF4I; "Lana Turner's Last Interview." YouTube video, 5:59. From *Lifestyles of the Rich and Famous*, September 1994. Posted by falconcrestblog, Januaray 2, 2010, https://www.youtube.com/watch?v=K5om-dbir0A.

38. "Lana Turner's Last Interview."

39. "Lana Turner's Last Interview."

40. "Lana Turner's Last Interview."

CHAPTER ELEVEN

1. A.C. Lyles, interview with author, June 15, 1992. A.C. started working at Paramount in 1928, shortly after his tenth birthday, and landed a job with studio head Adolph Zukor in 1936, soon rising to director of publicity and becoming a producer in 1953. He was best friends of James Cagney and Ronald Reagan and, at the time of his death on September 27, 2013, had worked at Paramount for eighty-five years—Paramount's longest-serving employee. I got to know A.C. when I was writing about Betty for *Newport Life Magazine.*

2. Robert Osbourne, "Private Screenings with Betty Hutton," interview, April 2000.

3. Betty Hutton obituary, *The Telegraph*, March 13, 2007.

4. "Private Screenings with Betty Hutton."

5. Betty Hutton, interview by Mike Douglas, *The Mike Douglas Show*, February 25, 1977.

6. Marian Christy, "Betty Hutton: I'm a Phoenix," *The Boston Globe*, December 10, 1986.

7. Betty Hutton, interview by Mike Douglas.

8. "Private Screenings with Betty Hutton."

9. Betty Hutton, interview by Mike Douglas.

10. Christy.

11. His year of his death is usually given, incorrectly, as 1939, but the date on his death certificate is August 26, 1937.

12. Christy.

13. "Private Screenings with Betty Hutton."

14. "This Side of Happiness," *Time Magazine*, April 24, 1950.

15. Betty Hutton, interview by Mike Douglas.

16. "Command Performance Strictly G.I. Part 1 of 2." YouTube video, 7:39. Posted by Historycomestolife, July 5, 2010, https://www.youtube.com/watch?v=1YNRgO5vlQ4.

17. Betty Hutton, with Carl Bruno and Michael Mayer, *Backstage You*

Can Have (Palm Springs, Calif.: The Betty Hutton Estate, 2009), pp. 263–265.

18. Hutton told Jay Sharbutt, *Associated Press*, on September 13, 1980, of her twenty year addiction, "It started when I was playing Vegas and found I was getting tired. The old snap wasn't there, the shows were too hard. My mother gave me a little tiny Dexamil (a stimulant).... It was innocent as that, and I said 'That's it! I'm not tired!'... It led to a vicious cycle, pills to get 'up,' pills to calm down."

19. "Remembering Betty Hutton: Good, Bad, Ugly Revealed about Musical Star of '40s," *The Desert Sun*, March 24, 2007.

20. "Remembering Betty Hutton."

21. Jay Sharbutt, "Bombshell Betty Hutton Hits Broadway in 'Annie,'" *Associated Press*, September 13, 1980.

22. Betty Hutton, interview by Mike Douglas.

23. Betty Hutton obituary, *The Independent* (London) March 14, 2007.

24. "Biography," The Betty Hutton Website, www.satinsandspurs.com/biography.

25. Betty Hutton obituary, *The Telegraph*, March 14, 2007.

26. Sharbutt, "Bombshell Betty Hutton."

27. Christy. "Fifteen years ago, I wanted to die," she said in this 1986 interview.

28. Elliot Krieger, "Betty Hutton Receives Degree at Salve Regina," *Providence Journal Bulletin*, September 30, 1984.

29. Jean Judge, "Ageless Betty Hutton: She's 'Right Up Front.'" *Fall River, Massachusetts Herald News*, September 21, 1982.

30. Judge, "Ageless Betty Hutton."

31. Judge, "Ageless Betty Hutton."

32. Professor James Hersh, interview with author, in the summer of 2007.

33. "Private Screenings with Betty Hutton." Though in *Boston Globe* interview, she states she called him and, "It was he who let me become the cook."

34. Christy.

35. Internet Movie Database Blog Post.

36. Christy.

37. Richard Severo, "Betty Hutton, Film Star of '40s and '50s, Dies at 86," *The New York Times*, March 13, 2007.

38. "Private Screenings with Betty Hutton."

39. "Private Screenings with Betty Hutton."

40. Elliott Krieger, "Betty Hutton receives degree at Salve Regina," *Providence Journal-Bulletin*, September 30, 1984.

41. Stephen Holden, "Pop: Reunion in Tribute to Capital." *The New York Times*, March 1982.

42. Barbara Polichetti, "Betty Hutton Moves to the Head of the Class," *Providence Journal*, May 19, 1986.

43. Thomas.

44. Hutton, *Backstage You Can Have*, p. 375.

45. Close friend of Betty Hutton who prefers to remain anonymous, interview with author.

CHAPTER TWELVE

1. Ann Miller and Norma Lee Browning, *Miller's High Life* (Garden City, N.Y.: Doubleday, 1972).

2. Frank Miller, "Ann Miller Profile," at TCM.com. This is a famous quote attributed to Ann Miller, perhaps her most famous quote, though the source is unclear.

3. Miller and Browning, p. 18.

4. Miller and Browning, p. 21.

5. Miller and Browning, pp. 15–16.

6. Miller and Browning, p. 37.

7. Miller and Browning, pp. 28–29.

8. Miller and Browning, p. 38.

9. Miller and Browning, p. 44.

10. Miller and Browning, p. 46.

11. Miller and Browning, p. 55.

12. Miller and Browning, p. 114.

13. Miller and Browning, p. 15.

14. Miller and Browning, p. 125.

15. Miller and Browning, p. 138.

16. Miller and Browning, pp. 241–242.

17. Miller and Browning, p. 22.

18. Miller and Browning, p. 21.

19. Fr. Loftus sits on the charitable foundation June and her husband, Fred MacMurray, set up.

20. Evelyn had come to work for Fr. Loftus in 1980, when he served at the Chancery as the diocesan point person for Catholic Charities. She was in her fifties when she began working for him and she stayed with him when he was subsequently asked to start a department at the chancery to organize a ministry for prisoners and juvenile delinquents. He described her as the most loyal person, not broaching even a scintilla of disparaging remarks, as is common about those in authority. She died of cancer in 2000. "I had been ministering to her," said Fr. Loftus. "And, June called and said she's not at all good today. And, I happened to have a funeral at Holy Cross, down near the airport. And, so I said, 'I'll do the funeral and I'll come along that way. And, I'll bring her communion and anoint her again and all the prayers and all that and spend a little time there.' She was very weak." As soon as he got back to St. Mel's, he said, "June phoned to say she just died. I was right with there almost to the last minute."

CHAPTER THIRTEEN

1. Mother Dolores, Prioress of the Abbey of Regina Laudis, was responding to my question at the Catholic Information Center, Washington, D.C., on June 6, 2013, where she was speaking about her newly published book, *The Ear of the Heart: An Actress' Journey from Hollywood to Holy Vows* (San Francisco: Ignatius, 2013).

2. Patricia Neal and Richard DeNeut, *As I Am: An Autobiography* (New York: Simon and Schuster, 1988), pp. 19 and 25.

3. Neal and DeNeut, p. 20.

4. Neal and DeNeut, p. 21.

5. Neal and DeNeut, pp. 35–36.

6. Neal and DeNeut, p. 32.

7. Robert Osbourne, "Private Screenings with Patricia Neal," Turner Classic Movies, April 2004.

8. Neal and DeNeut, p. 40.

9. Neal and DeNeut, pp. 50–52.

10. Neal and DeNeut, p. 58.

11. "Private Screenings with Patricia Neal."

12. Neal and DeNeut, pp. 59–63.

13. Neal and DeNeut, p. 125.

14. Mother Dolores.

15. Stephen Michael Shearer, *Patricia Neal: An Unquiet Life* (Lexington, Ky.: The University Press of Kentucky, 2006).

16. Neal and DeNeut, p. 106.

17. Neal and DeNeut, p. 126.

18. Neal and DeNeut, photo 36 caption and p. 129.

19. Neal and DeNeut, pp. 254 and 256.

20. Neal and DeNeut, p. 276.

21. Neal and DeNeut, p. 276.

22. Neal and DeNeut, p. 288.

23. Neal and DeNeut, p. 287.

24. Neal and DeNeut, p. 294.

25. Neal and DeNeut, p. 305.

26. Orphelia Dahl, Executive Director, Partners in Health, interview with author, August 2012.

27. Now known as the Fort Sanders Regional Medical Center, it is distinguished for its work in stroke rehabilitation, and also helps victims of spinal cord, brain, traumatic brain, and orthopedic injuries, as well as cancer.

28. Neal and DeNeut, p. 319.

29. Neal and DeNeut, pp. 322–323.

30. Neal and DeNeut, p. 345.

31. Mother Dolores.

32. Neal and DeNeut, p. 346.

33. Neal and DeNeut, p. 347.

34. Maria Cooper Janis, interview with author, August 2011.

35. Neal and DeNeut, pp. 347–351.

36. Neal and DeNeut, p. 355.

37. "Private Screenings with Patricia Neal."

38. Mother Dolores.

39. Mother Dolores.

40. Mother Dolores.

CONCLUSION

1. Thomas.

2. Cardinal Sergio Pignedoli, "Divine Ways on Earth: St. Josemaria Escriva de Balaguer" (New Rochelle, N.Y.: Scepter, 1976).

3. Raphael Brown, trans. and ed., *The Little Flowers of St. Francis* (New York: Doubleday, 1958), pp. 319–320.